A Story of the Heavenly Camp-Fires

CONTENTS

A STORY OF

THE HEAVENLY CAMP-FIRES

INTRODUCTORY

I

WE are they "who only stand and wait," but we wait to do our Master's bidding; and while we wait we tell experiences of our new condition,— and often we are sent to cheer the hearts of others who have not yet come hither. If we are militant in no earthly sense, but rather ministrant, yet in our world celestial we speak of earth as a field of battle, in which many valiant spirits are sore wounded; and if we go to bind up their wounds, and cheer them for new contests, we say that we, who dwell in the realms of perfect peace, have been to engage in conflict,—when we have not been in the fight, unless to help those who are wounded. It is much, indeed, like what we used to call the Red Cross League or Commission service; in which many of us were wont to serve, before we crossed the silver stream, that divides our old abode from the new.

I cannot, in telling those stories, refer to any story-teller by his heavenly name, which cannot be translated into the language of the earth; nor does any one wish to be called by his earthly name, unless by domestic friends at their coming. Their old names, they say, were connected with much that was displeasing to God; and they are no longer pleased with them. Even those whose names are prefixed by "Saint," upon the earth, or who were known as "Church" Fathers, or "pillars" in the Church, are now so sensitive about many things that they ought to have been ashamed of on the earth, that they do not like to be reminded of their old names, so tarnished in their own eyes. And authors once of some repute do not care to be reminded of their old names, once famous among people whose spiritual ideals are formed on imperfect models.

Unless in rare instances, I can best designate the story-tellers by their earthly employments or conditions, of which every one is proud; since all are now content with their individual lots before coming here. In the light, which we now dwell in, we can see that what we were and what we aimed for in our former estate was ordered by Divine Love; and now we never quarrel in our hearts with the infinite love of God, or distrust his care of us, whether in days present or past. Indeed, all our burdens are gone, and we feel happiest of all that we have now definitely laid aside the work of attempting to govern

the universe, which we once sought to do,—at
least so far as concerned our place in it; and
this is the reason why we say now, I was a shoe-
maker, and I wear a golden hammer for my
badge,—I never cheated at shoemaking, and I
am proud of my old occupation. Or one says, I
used to do domestic work, and make clean corners for women who could not well do it for
themselves; and now I wear a golden broom for
my badge, and I am proud of it. I was never an
eye-servant. I lived as seeing Him who is Invisible.

And so, all through the category of earthly
service, there is no one but takes pride in what
he did, since he did it as unto God. Even the
princes and kings of the earth are not ashamed
of having had honor among men; although they
do not wear coronets or any insignia of royalty
here; this is because they have heard that un-
repentant kings in their spiritual realms make
much ado about their rank. Such royal personages as are here, commonly wear badges taken
from some person they helped in their earthly
condition. A Prince of Poland now knows that
the one great act of his Polish life, was when he
befriended a miner; and he wears a golden pick
upon his breast.

I cannot in these tales say what relates to myself. I am a new-comer, and have not recovered

from the *furor scribendi*, from which I suffered when upon the earth. I have written what I have heard; but have reflected so little upon my own story, that I am not ready to tell it to my wise comrades. They would laugh at my self-conceit; which, however, I am losing every day.

The first tale is that of a poet, who once lived on a beautiful island amid stormy seas.

II

Sitting upon the greensward, at our twilight fire, upon the banks of a rill running into the River of Life, it was hard for us to recall the circumstances of the earth, so far as to make vivid the scenes he depicted. It was like calling up the imagery of a dream :—

"'The nightingale sings sweetest, when it urgeth its breast with a thorn:' at least, so I used to hear when I was a child. But whether it be so, I do not know. My poetic license, taken out in the time of King Alfred, did not require me to observe the facts in natural history, and I never did, till I came to this country. And as for nightingales, I have studiously avoided them here, since the first one I heard seemed to mock me for the so-called poem I once made in Kent upon the nightingale, in which I grossly misrepresented the facts as to the habits of the bird.

This, however, has all gone by; and I should not have thought of it, but for this proverb, which illustrates what I was about to observe in regard to the Land of Shadows from which I think we all came."

Having said this, he cautiously peered about a little to see whether indeed there were any comrades present, who were not earth-born. Having satisfied himself upon this point, he proceeded :—

"Those who have been here longest are so much better informed than I am, that I shrink a little from talking too much, lest I bring discredit to my native place, and dishearten our Kent county club, which is seeking to rid us all from our provincial limitations. But I see there is no one present who has been here so long as I have, so that I am as free to display my half-knowledge, as if I were still upon that happy isle between rough seas.

"If I speak relatively,—you will understand me : it is a tolerably happy isle. The most part of our time here, we seek for the new, without dwelling upon the old; still our new knowledge has to be attached to the old, I fancy,—or it would not adhere. While now we are off duty, let us tell the tales of the Land of Shadow. Is not the earth fitly termed the Land of Shadow ?"

"It is," I made bold to answer; "but it is the Shadow of our Father's Hand."

"Very good, be it so," the poet replied. "For
if I were to sum up all I know about the earth,
and what I now know about the outcome of
earthly discipline, I should say, that human life
is one long woe, struggling with adverse circumstances."

"You mean," said one who wore an anchor on
his breast, "that 'a smooth sea never made a
good sailor.'"

"Yes; and then, too, I mean to qualify my
affirmation. Some of the woes are imaginary,—
conjured up by morbid mental condition; yet the
people most favored, have trouble enough of
some sort, at some time, to make good my prop-
osition that, on the whole, human life is one long
woe, struggling with adverse circumstances."

"You will, I am sure, qualify that still more,"
I said. "You remember the old saw, 'Merry
as an Englishman.'"

"That's true," answered the poet; "they used
to say 'Merry England,' when I lived there."

"And you know," said an African, "what
happy times our people used to have; that is,—
whenever our circumstances allowed it."

"And we too," chimed in a native of one of
the Greek isles.

"I acknowledge all that," the poet replied.
"I used to think that, for pure animal joy,
the children in Kent were much happier than

the colts and the calves. But what I mean is still true. I did not know it, till I came here. Yet some centuries of heaven have satisfied me that there is so much alloy in human happiness, ,that to me the earth is a Land of Shadow, the shadow indeed of our Father's Hand."

"Very good," we all cried; "we will agree to that."

There was only a small group, about our evening fire; and we were well agreed not to quarrel with the young poet, who was, by some generations, older than most of us.

"I wish," resumed the man of Kent, who, by-the-way, wore a golden plow for a badge upon his girdle, "I wish that I could put my words into metric form, for your delectation; but the truth is that I gave up poetry hundreds of years ago. I made 'commendable poetry' till I was tired of it. My poetic feet were all right, but I never had a poetic spirit, or any poetic ideas; so that you will excuse me, if I tell my tale in prose."

"How many hundreds of years did it take you to find out that you could not write poetry?" I asked.

"Three," he replied. "My so-called poetic era I look upon, as I used to look upon children when teething, or when they had the mumps. I had to have it,—but I've got over it now; and am reasonably well, so far as I know.

"I fear, however," he added, "that I shall never get at my story, if you interrupt me any further."

"Haven't you 'all eternity' to tell it in?" I ventured to ask.

"That is true, if you have nothing else to do than to listen."

III

"It is little that I would say," he continued, "save that I think of human life upon the earth, as swamped in a sea of sorrows: the conditions necessarily make it so. It is figured by what happens to the physical globe itself, which is, constitutionally, in constant change:—

"The loss of heat causes the earth to contract; then gravitation draws the rocky earth-crust inward,—so generating more heat. These earth movements keep the surface irregular; and they counteract the constant disintegration and degradation of the land by frost and sunshine and rain. Whenever the earth is completely condensed, these energies will cease to work; and the earth will be lifeless as the moon.

"So human life is always being built up and torn down. One generation goeth and another cometh: this means hundreds of millions of heart-breakings in every generation; it means disease; it means poverty. Then too, these generations are so far animals as to have instincts, appetites, and passions, that easily degenerate into the brutal: this means crime, tyranny, warfare, oppression.

"When I lived in Kent, they used to say that the grim Scythians celebrated the birth of infants, as they would funerals. 'I wept when I was born, and every day shows why': that is what my mother used to say. And Shakspere said,—as I have been told,—that

"'One woe doth tread upon another's heel.'

"Yet I used to observe, on my farm, that winter, which kills the flower, often helps the root. And it is one of the prerogatives of the strong to suffer. Some late poet has said, that we ought to praise God

"'For the pleasant corn and wine,
    And summer heat; and also for
    The frost upon the sycamore,
    And hail upon the vine.'

"And a plowman from Kent County has also sung in recent days :—

"'O bright, with sunlight gleams,
    Are all our sorrow streams :

Our crags, our rills,—
The oak, the fir, the pine,
The corn, the fruit, the vine,—
Of nature's tears the sign—
Life's gain from ills.'

"All the material for poetry would be taken away from the world at once, if there were no adverse circumstances to contend with."

"I know that to be true," interrupted the Greek. "And I count it one of the great felicities of my celestial life, that I have finally found out about Prometheus, and Hercules. I used to be a very ignorant man, having been a fisher-boy. But since I came here, I have conversed with several very learned critics; and now I have found out what the poets had to go upon. I always admired the lines, so apt upon the earth, so strange to heaven :—

"' They see above them sailing
O'er life's barren crags the vulture.'

But I've been told that Prometheus was only a more enterprising seafaring man than I was, and that when he saw the sea's horizon, he boldly made for it; and then sailed so far as to discover new constellations,—so stealing fire from heaven ; then he was wrecked, and rock bound, —and he was gnawed by hunger."

"Yet what magnificent material for poetry,"

added the Kentish plowman. "The poet said he was bound on Caucasus ten thousand years, for stealing that fire, to help men.

> " ' Thou shalt long
> For starry-mantled night to hide day's sheen,
> For sun to melt the rime of early dawn.'

> " ' Thou still shalt keep thy watch, nor lying down,
> Nor knowing sleep, nor ever bending knee;
> And many groans and wailings profitless
> Thy lips shall utter; for the mind of Zeus
> Remains inexorable.' "

"And then there was Hercules," continued the Greek, "who was another enterprising ship-master in the youth of the world. He went out, and rescued Prometheus. He passed the hydra-headed promontories; and burned their heads with fire, by kindling beacon lights upon them. He went out through the pillars of Hercules, and discovered golden apples in tropical gardens; and he went ashore on some foreign continent, and captured various wild beasts. And on his return, he invented a sanitary system of sewage. I don't wonder that our people deified him. But they never would have done it, if he had not been so plucky in overcoming the adverse circumstances that beset him."

"There's another thing," remarked the man of Kent. "It is proved to be true that 'time'

is but a piece of 'eternity.' It is the beginning
of the timeless eons. And those who suffer sorrow on earth may well say, with Philip of Mace-
don, 'Time and I against any two.' When I
once left the earth, I had a chance to do something besides plowing, and writing poetry on all
subjects for neighborhood occasions."

At this point King Alfred the Great came in:
and learning the trend of our conversation, he
was pleased to add, that "There are many phenomena in nature, concerning which we have at
first little conception of their design; and it is
so, as to many of the events in our earthly lives.
We have learned more, in later ages."

Then the Kentish plowman closed our fireside
talk with a snatch of what I suppose was one of
his commendable poems, without metric form:—

"He must see a night, who would see the stars. By
day is seen one sun; and the vision is full of the near
earth, and its beauty. By night are seen ten thousand
suns; and the vision is full of the far heavens, and infin-
itude of beauty."

Before breaking up, however, we agreed that
we would continue our fireside tales concerning
the Land of Shadow, so dear to us; and that we
would see, if possible, whether it were not the
Shadow of our Father's Hand; and that we would
also see whether our Father's Hand were not very

near to the earth, in order to lead the people away from the Shadow into the Light of our Father's House. And good King Alfred said, that he would tell the first story, at the next evening fire.

Book 1

SHADOW OF OUR FATHER'S HAND

Book 1

THE SHADOW OF OUR FATHER'S HAND

CHAPTER FIRST

I

IT was, however, several days before we all got together again. Meantime, some went one way and some another, on various errands of mercy. King Alfred went to Armenia; and I almost wish that he could have stayed, and been the king of that country. Our next camp-fire was kindled upon the edge of a table mountain of great height, looking far away toward the City of the Great King, whose light was like that of the Day illuminating the fringes of the Night. There is no night in the sense of darkness or sorrow or need of repose; but there are twilight hours for quiet communion with God, and for social and domestic gatherings, when celestial employments are laid aside, and either in silence or in society every one takes time to contemplate his happiness in being in a world where the wicked cease from troubling, and the weary are at rest.

A certain dignity of mien and ineffable spirituality of countenance is noticed among those who have been in these realms of immortality for some centuries; and they appear much more youthful than those who have but lately laid aside the anxieties of earth. Still I was not prepared to see one with marks of adolescence so apparent as in King Alfred; he bids fair, indeed, to live forever, and to become still younger in look, since he is always approaching the likeness of the Self-Existent One.

"You must remember," he said, "that the harp is derived from the bow of the archer, and that a bow-string was the first musician. Whenever I go to England now, I visit some old battle-ground there, to gather a wild rose, or some token that peace reigns where I once saw brethren contend. It was a great many years, indeed many centuries, in which British soil was soaked in the blood of her own sons, for petty or gigantic grievances. It took one whole generation to kill off the heads of the great feudal houses, and the land was the better for it. The sharp struggles for civil and for religious freedom caused every man, in building the state, to bear in one hand a weapon. And I have noticed, in observing the course of English history, that liberty gained most during long reigns of wicked but weak kings, in which the people taught the throne to redress their grievances; this being the price royalty had to pay to the commons for the means of carrying on the government. So that whenever the torch of freedom was reversed, it was only to burn the more fiercely."

At this point the speaker was interrupted by the arrival of Gustavus Adolphus, in search for the British king. He participated, however, for a moment in the discussion of our fireside topic, saying :

"I can but smile at one of the sovereigns of Great Britain, who desired to have her portrait painted without a shadow on the canvas. Having had no small experience as an artist in my life celestial, I have never succeeded in painting the battle-scenes of the Thirty Years' War without dark blotches of shade; and my statue of Civil Liberty has massive limbs, won by struggling. National trials educate the whole people, and lead them to think of the principles of justice and religion which underlie liberty. A war for an idea teaches men to think. The pool at Bethesda could not heal without being first disturbed. The reflux in the advancing tide is because of the life and force of the sea. Every living movement has ebbing moments. Agitation is the life of liberty. The day of peace can come only after the awful night of battle.

"When I have completed the painting I am at work on now, I trust that you will all come and see it. Knowing what I do about the course

of events in the Land of Shadow, what subject
could I have chosen so fit as this : it is the figure
of Human Wrath praising God.   The great wrath
of man shall at last praise God, and the praise
shall be loud, and the universe shall hear it, and
heaven shall record it, and hell shall tremble at
the sound thereof.   Among the countless living
creatures that on some high festal day crowd
into the City of the Great King, there stands
the bloody Wrath of Man saying, 'Blessing and
honor and glory and power be unto Him that
sitteth on the throne, and to the Lamb, for ever
and ever.'"

II

King Alfred and the King of Sweden now
bade us follow them ; and, as swiftly as the light,
we reached another camp-fire down the mountain
side, in a grove of fir-trees, upon the banks of a
swift stream.   Here we found a little company
who had gathered to discuss the question of
God's persecuted saints upon the earth, and they
were looking for King Alfred's report of what he
had lately seen.

Being made welcome to their company, we now
saw that John Milton stood foremost,—he who left
his Italian studies to hasten home, when the little
isle between rough seas was rocked by savage war.

"If any one asks me," he said, "what is my opinion of events now transpiring in the Land of Shadow, I make bold to say that when the devil of tyranny hath gone into the body politic in any land, he departs not but with struggles and foaming and great convulsions. Shall he vex it forever, lest, in going out, he for a moment tear and rend it? We have sometimes engaged in war from absolute necessity against those who would not allow us to be at peace with them. And if such deluge passes over a nation, washing away ancient landmarks, and sweeping away dwellings, and giving birth to foul and dangerous reptiles, yet, like the blessed flood of the Nile, we find in it the fulness of the granary, the beauty of the garden, the nurture of all living things. It is certain that they who by their labors, counsels, and prayers, have been earnest for the common good, shall receive above the inferior orders of the blessed in the Light of our Father's House; and in supereminence of beatific vision, shall clasp inseparable hands, with joy and bliss in over-measure forever."

Upon this Oliver Cromwell spoke:

"Who could have forethought, when we were plunged into the midst of our Ten Years' War, that ever the people of God should have had liberty to worship God without fear of enemies? War is always better than a wicked peace.

'Shall we,' asked John Calvin, 'to save life, forsake the Author of existence ? To have peace with men, shall we make war with God ?' Better rather, as Jeremiah has said, better rather 'set up a standard in the land, and blow the trumpet among the nations. O thou sword of the Lord, how long will it be ere thou be quiet ? Put up thyself into thy scabbard, rest, and be still. How can it be quiet, seeing the Lord hath given it a charge ? The daughter of Babylon is a threshing-floor; it is time to thresh her.' If nothing should ever be done but what is according to law, the throat of the nation may be cut while we send for some one to make a law. 'Thou hast girded me with strength for the battle,' quoth David, in the eighteenth Psalm. I am of the opinion, that the kingdom of God is to the strongest; and that there are considerable areas of the Land of Shadow to-day where they need to have things settled. I stand for a settlement. I would take many a fine city, and fulfil the saying of the prophet of the Almighty,—'I will wipe Jerusalem as a man wipeth a dish; wiping it, and turning it upside down.'"

I now observed a silent man, standing with his back against a great fir. It was William of Orange, whose untimely death eclipsed half the world. He had lived in "a made-up country, in which life or death depend on a hole made in a dyke." As vast subterranean forces energize volcanic ranges, so the iniquitous plans of the under-world found vent on the low-lying shores of the German Ocean, deluging a hundred thousand Christians with fire. Up rose this silent man, — "I maintain." And freedom was maintained at the expense of eighty years of war.

"War," he said, "is at times a purifier. It is like a thunder-storm, which drives off the pestilence; its bolt kills one family, the pestilence would kill a thousand men. I stand for war, when it is a conflict for law, for order, for the obligation of solemn compacts; for the sanctity of oaths; for religion, for morality, for social quiet; for all that secures the transmission of healthy political institutions from age to age; for all that is venerable in history; for all that is lovely, pure, peaceable, and of good report among men; for all that truly makes government a power ordained of God."

"While I am slow to counsel war," now responded he whom I had recognized as first in the hearts of my own countrymen, "yet I advise it, if it be in the cause of virtue and freedom; having, however, fair conditions for success in the contest. We are to learn of conditions from the Messenger."

As we now withdrew, lest we intrude upon the consultations to follow, I heard the voice of a poet familiar to me, but whose face I did not see :

"I have seen that great desolation, when the shops were silent, when muscular men were forced to depend on charity, when those who should have tilled the soil were upon the distant battle-field defending their right to toil in peace, when merchantmen furled their sails and privateers scoured the seas.   Yet —

"Down the dark future, through the long generations,
   The sounds of war grow fainter, then cease ;
And like a bell with solemn, sweet vibrations,
   I hear the voice of Christ say—'Peace.'"

III

The straitened ideas of heaven I used to have when I lived in the Land of Shadow, underwent a great shock when I first entered the Light of our Father's House.   The first stranger I met in this country was one of my present comrades, the Kentish plowman ; and he had it all figured out in black and white.

"When I came here," he said, "I was greatly surprised to find that heaven is a much larger place than the entire county of Kent.   I afterwards found out that there are more than a hundred million suns in the material universe as it is now; and that on an average there is at least one inhabited planet to every sun system, some suns having several peopled worlds and others none.   There are at a low estimate a thousand million, million, millions of people to be provided for in the heavenly world : a hundred million planets, averaging ten hundred millions of people in every generation, during ten thousand generations averaging a hundred years each,—since those planets average each a million years as their period of habitability.

"Now, I never thought of this when I lived in Kent.   I always thought heaven was like London, only bigger, without any smoke, or fog, or dirt, or deceit, or wickedness.   After I arrived, as you have just come now, I found that a thousand million, million, millions of people require more room than Kent and London.   As a matter of convenience in housing so many people, they are distributed throughout a system of spheres connected with a central body.   It is a heavenly suburban system, with planetary globes and a central orb, and the inhabitants pass from one to another with the speed of light."

My present object in alluding to this bit of Kentish information is to explain how it comes about that we have twilight in the suburban spheres of the heavenly world. At twilight, those who are so minded have their camp-fires, as we do now when on duty.

At our next camp-fire, we resumed our conversation concerning the Shadow of our Father's Hand which covers our old home, the earth. "It is plain enough," remarked the plowman, "from what we heard last evening, that what I have said is true, that human life is one long woe, struggling with adverse circumstances."

"I have been surprised since I came here," said the Greek sailor, "to find out that God's providence uses man's activity to forward divine purposes. I always thought that Alexander the Great and Julius Cæsar were simple servants of the devil, but the Lord of Hosts had a use for them. It seems strange enough to us, that the soldiers of Alexander dying in the East should have affected our destiny; yet the blood which flowed in breaking up the Asiatic despotisms aided in preparing the world for the coming of Christ. Plutarch, you know, has said that Alexander did not harken to his preceptor Aristotle, in his treatment of the barbarians; but, conceiving that he was sent by God to be an umpire between all, and to unite all together, he formed of a hundred diverse nations one single universal body, mingling as it were in one cup the friendship, the customs, and the laws of all; he desired that all should regard the whole world as their own country."

"Yea, too," said Dante, the poet, who had come among us unobserved, "and the armies of Rome were but the hammers of God, to level the kingdoms of the world, to prepare for the Kingdom of Christ. It took five hundred years for Rome to subdue Italy; and after that, the city came to rule a hundred and twenty millions of people. And the barbaric nations were benefited by being conquered. The culture and the laws of Italy were borne to Spain and Gaul and Britain; and the resources of the provinces were developed as they never had been by their ancient kings.

"Our Lord endows men with strong will and invincible energy, and gives them authority upon the earth; and those mighty men wish, as Pindar said, to tread the floors of hell on necessities as hard as iron. Their adversities are great, until they become great in their adversities. It is through struggling, and through bitter suffering, that the best worth of the world is made."

The great Italian, who has now achieved such fame as a poet in the celestial country, was much more gracious and companionable than he used to be in the Land of Shadow; and we detained him long, listening to the harmonious numbers that fell from his lips. And it was only after Dante's departure that our poet from Kent ventured to speak; and then it was not in verse.

"To take up the topic again," he remarked, "I have noticed that the men of the Land of Shadow learn much through their contending with adverse circumstances. London learned to build better, after a broom of fire swept the city clean."

"And I too have noticed," I said, "that the famines and fires of the earth do much to develop human brotherhood and mutual helpfulness. The misery, the physical wretchedness, and spiritual degradation of vast populations call out Christ-like charities; and the angelic faculties are put into training, and the earth is in a certain measure made like heaven."

V

And now the light was strongly increasing, and we could see the vast table-land on the mountain-top quite alive with gathering squadrons, whose shining lances were gleaming in the light of the new day. They were under the charge of a Roman centurion, who was disciplining certain raw recruits among the hosts of heaven. I overhead him expounding certain texts in the Chronicles and the Prophets : "Such as went forth to battle, who were expert in war, who could keep rank, who were not of double heart. It is said, Neither shall one thrust another, they shall walk every one in his path. And it is written that none shall stumble among them, and that none shall slumber nor sleep; and that they shall run like mighty men and climb the wall like men of war."

He taught them to keep the munition, to watch the way, to fortify strongholds, and put captains in them, and store of victuals.

"I would have you know," spoke the centurion, "that so long as a vigorous barbarism, and a selfish ambition, and great avarice, remain upon the earth, it is our duty to be ready to fight. So that, whenever God shall speak concerning a kingdom, to pluck up, and to pull down, and to destroy it, we may be ready."

VI

It is fitting to say, at this point in my story, that the thousand million, million, millions of the inhabitants of heaven have a diversity of drill and employment. This sphere, where I am at this moment, is but part of that heaven-system, which is widely separated from the material universe that is known to earthly astronomers. This sphere, where I am, is indeed one of the mansions of our Father's house. Yet it is occupied just now as a primary school, for the discipline and the training of inhabitants of the Land of Shadow who come hither. We have among us a vast number of teachers, who were earth-born, who have lived upon other spheres of intermediate, or high-school, or collegiate, or university grades; although this is not as these grades are called in the heavenly language. And we often make excursions hither and thither to these different spheres of light.

And it is one of the features of the work we are taught to do in the primary sphere, that what we learn is attached to what we learned and what we most needed to learn before we came here. The Kentish plowman told me that the Roman centurion was of great service to him, in teaching him to hold his head up, and to keep

his shoulders back, and to have a more manly
bearing than he used to have on his farm.   And
there have been soldiers not a few, well trained
here, who have been of earthly service at critical
junctures in the advancement of the Kingdom
of God in our dear Land of Shadow.

To accommodate the numbers without number who are constantly coming to the heavenly
system from a hundred million planets of what
is known to earth as the material universe, it is a
matter of convenience to classify them at first
according to the planets they come from.   Those
who come from the earth, come here, where I
am now.   Here they meet their acquaintances
and kinsfolk, and here they carry on life in the
Light of our Father's House, instead of struggling along as they used to do in the Land of
Shadow.   Then, as they advance in knowledge, and their dear ones are gathered about
them, there are vast family removals to some
other heavenly sphere where they may gain new
experiences in a divine life.   Yet in all spheres
the light of God is everywhere.   It is all heaven.
And everywhere we join in hymns of thanksgiving.

It seems dreadful in such a place to talk about
war, and the barbarisms of the Land of Shadow.
And the angels of God, or the spirits of just
men made perfect, who were born in some dis-

3

tant part of the material universe, perhaps in
Orion, or the Southern Cross, sometimes visit
our camp-fires in sad wonder at the tales we tell,
of sinning and repenting, of sorrow and death,
concerning which they know so little.

CHAPTER SECOND

I

NOTHING has surprised me in this country so much as the different aspect of earthly things when seen from the heavenly standpoint. It is like looking at gorgeously painted windows, when seen from the right rather than the wrong side. Dark shadows, which seem only daubs of blood disfiguring the scene, appear as the most effective parts of the painting when God's sunlight shines through the transparency. The conception I formed of heaven, when I was upon the earth, proved to be almost altogether erroneous. To imagine what heaven is like, as thought of from an earthly standpoint, is utterly misleading. But now that I am in position to judge of earthly things from a celestial vantage-ground, I can never be weary of reviewing the situation. It is much like untying the tangles of the mundane sphere; and I can now see the true meaning of human history in its broad relations, and in its particular events, so far as they are known to me.

Our various duties kept us apart for a long

time following the conversation last reported; and when we next kindled our camp-fire, we had for our guest that doughty old puritan, Richard Baxter. I never saw a man more changed in my life. That is, he was not what I had supposed him to be. I thought I knew how he would look. I had read his innumerable books,— so polemical, practical, and prolix. Yet now he bore no mark of his times, or of his sufferings in the cause of God. Indeed I have never met one of the earth-born angels more youthful in mien than he, or one more in accord with all that is best in the modern age. He is so indefatigable a student that he keeps himself in spare condition; but he is so well knit in his make-up that he would be formidable to meet, when going forth as an angel militant.

He fell in at once with our project to debate the adverse circumstances of earthly condition, as seen in the light of eternity; and he claimed that all manly qualities were the better for hard contending in the Land of Shadow.

"What blessings have rained on the earthly Church," he said, "have come by their being under a cloud. I noticed at Kidderminster that the clouds were great storehouses over our heads, full of corn. And it was apparent in the warm season that cloudy nights were more favorable to growth than those that were starlighted. My

house plants I often shut up for a little time
in the damp and the dark.   Ceaseless sunshine
parches.   Then, too, the true Church has been
kept poor,—having nothing but God."

I could but recall, as I listened to him, his
going to prison when he was seventy years old,
for the cause of religious toleration; and I could
but recall his quaintly phrased thanksgiving to
God for his earthly trials and discipline: "How
safe is this, in comparison of full prosperity and
pleasure."   Much as he endured for conscience'
sake, and much in physical afflictions, he thought
about it now little more than a man in his prime
is always attempting to recall his experiences as
an infant.   The serene centuries of heaven had
nothing in them to disturb his tranquillity of
spirit.

"I have been interested," he said, "in Lord
Bacon's remark that the pencil of the Holy
Ghost labored more in describing the afflictions
of Job than the felicities of Solomon; and that
if we listen to David's harp, we shall hear as
many hearse-like airs as carols.   In very truth,
the Church of God has taken honey out of the
rock, and oil out of the flinty rock.   The nomad-
ic children of Israel were prepared for national
life by their generations of bondage in Egypt;
and the spiritless slaves were awakened in the
desert.   Egypt and the wilderness and Babylon

were the academies of Israel. The Lord gave to
his people the bread of adversity and the water
of affliction.

"When we have read all books, and examined
all methods, to find out the path that will lead
men out of the Land of Shadow into the Light
of our Father's House, this conclusion only will
remain : that through much tribulation we must
enter into the Kingdom of God. I will bring, it
is written, a third part through the fire, and will
refine them as silver is refined, and will try them
as gold is tried."

II

At the next twilight hour, we all accepted an
invitation to be present at a Reunion of the
Christian martyrs of the early centuries of the
Church of God on earth. And when we saw
their shining faces, we could but be a little sad-
dened that we too had not been privileged to
be burned, or torn by wild beasts.

It was in a mountain amphitheatre, with a
level floor. St. Perpetua presided,—being almost
the only one whose earthly name still clings to
her ; and here in the heavens, as once upon the
earth, every one is glad to call her a saint. The
prizes of the heavenly realm have not been
awarded to the rich who gave away all their

goods, nor to the learned who defended the Church, nor even to the apostolic missioners in every land, nor to those who laid down their lives for the faith; but they have been allotted to persons relatively obscure, and perhaps altogether unknown upon the earth, in whose hearts God discerned the brightest reflection of his own image.

It was notable in this vast gathering of the martyrs of the Church, that they all bore in their bodies the marks of the Lord Jesus, as having suffered for him. The assembly of martyrs occupied the level arena, while the mountains on every side were crowded with spectators; and we could see our Lord among them. Their words were as easily heard as if we had been in the midst of their company; and we saw them clearly from the crag where we were seated. I heard the voice of St. Perpetua:

"We were condemned to the wild beasts; and with hearts full of joy returned to our prison."

Not far from where we were sitting, I observed the Anglican bishop, Jeremy Taylor, in conversation with the Elector of Saxony, who signed the Augsburg confession, and Wolfgang, the ruler of Anhalt.

"The early Church," remarked the bishop, "went through ten persecutions; but the more they were afflicted, the more they multiplied and

grew. If we had seen St. Polycarp burning to
death, or St. Lawrence roasting upon his gridiron, or St. Ignatius exposed to lions, or St.
Sebastian pierced with arrows, or St. Attalus
carried about the theatre with scorn unto his
death, for the cause of Jesus, for religion, for
God, and a holy conscience,—we should have
been in love with flames, and have thought the
gridiron fairer than the ribs of a martial bed;
and we should have chosen to converse with
those beasts, rather than those men that brought
those beasts forth; and estimated the arrows to
be rays of light brighter than the moon; and
that disgrace and mistaken pageantry were a
solemnity richer and more magnificent than Mor-
decai's procession upon the king's horse, and in
the robes of majesty: for so did these holy men
account them; they kissed their stakes, and
hugged their deaths, and ran violently to tor-
ments, and counted whippings and secular dis-
graces to be the enamel of their persons and the
ointment of their heads and the embalming of
their names and securing them for immortality."

The Elector of Saxony wore, as I noticed, a
massive cross of gold. He it was who had once
said, in the Land of Shadow: "I desire to confess my Lord. My electoral hat and my ermine
are not so precious to me as the cross of Jesus
Christ. I shall leave on earth these marks of

my greatness; but my Master's cross will accompany me to heaven."

And I could not but with admiration look upon the crown of gold that brightened the black locks of Anhalt; and I saw that he wore the symbol of a pen upon his girdle. It was then that I recalled, how he signed his confession of faith, saying: "I have tilted more than once to please others; now, if the honor of my Lord Jesus Christ requires it, I am ready to saddle my horse, to leave my goods and my life behind, and to rush into eternity towards an everlasting crown."

I had not observed till now, that Theodore Beza was standing against a great oak upon our left; and I overheard him saying to Erasmus,— "The Church of God upon the earth has had to bear blows rather than to give them; but it is an anvil that has worn out many hammers."

"Burned, but not confuted," was the learned professor's reply. "It was no harm that men were burned, so long as they were not confuted."

My elbow was now sharply pulled by my comrade of Kent. He pointed out to me, in the arena below, Hugh Latimer. "It was my angelic mission," said the plowman, "to attend upon his martyrdom, and guide him hither. 'Dear brother,' I heard him say to one who suffered with him, 'let us rejoice and be glad; for

we shall this day help light such a candle in
England as by God's grace shall never be put
out.' And the candle is still burning."

III

At our next camp-fire, we had for our teachers
in the story of the earth Samuel Rutherford and
St. Chrysostom. The eloquent John of Antioch
is to-day the pride of myriads upon our sphere;
and yet he is as humble, and as easily accessible
as a little child. And of Rutherford, as I have
known him here, I can never say too much.

"The silent cells of God's suffering saints,"
said Rutherford, "have been gladdened by the
still small voice of the Divine Comforter. In
my own bonds how sweet and comfortable were
the thoughts of God to me, wherein I found
a sufficient recompense of reward. How blind
were my adversaries who sent me to a banquet-
ing-house with the Lord Jesus, and not to a
prison, or place of exile."

"Even in our heavenly hill-country," said the
golden-mouthed orator, "the chief glory of our
mountains is found in their storms or in their
robes of snow. The places of the most exceeding beauty are those locked between scarred
peaks. So God has adorned his chosen people

upon the earth by surrounding them with the awful scenery of sorrow; yet it is God who thus surrounds them.   It is *Via crucis, via lucis:* the way of the cross is the way of light.   ' As many as I love, I rebuke and chasten.'   He who has never known sorrow, neither knows man nor God.   Infinite Love has approved for every disciple of Christ what Infinite Wisdom has chosen, —his cross; prepared in the foreordaining mind of God.   It is the shadow of our Father's hand appointed to lead his child to the Light of our Father's House."

"I believe," remarked my comrade of Kent, after our guests had departed, "that a crown would crush a man too weak to carry a cross."

"And I remember," added the Greek sailor, " that rough gales always quicken the homeward bound."

CHAPTER THIRD

I

AFTER this, our conversation drifted towards that which characterizes individual experience, rather than great general movements, like national life, or that of the Church. Still, we could but think of the minor subdivisions of society, or group of workers in different callings. And we concluded that since our own experience in the Land of Shadow had been so brief, and since some of us had been quite pinched there, in the range of our studies, it would be a happy thought to invite to our camp-fire certain guests whose earthly lives had been far different from our own.

This plan seemed the more feasible, since everybody in this land is at leisure to be spoken with. No gaunt figure of death is skulking along near philosophers and students, to strike at them before their work is done. And the thousand necessities, that made their hours priceless in the Land of Shadow, have now gone by forever. Even the Son of Man who felt the

need of working while the day lasted in Galilee
and Judea, is now at leisure to be spoken with,—
the shadow of the cross no longer falls across
his path; and eternity is a long time to work in,
and every one who loves him is sure some time
to be alone with him.   Nor can I think without
tears of that hour, when I can tell him alone,—
"Thou knowest me altogether, and Thou knowest that I love Thee."

For our first guest, under this new arrange-
ment, we invited Sir Isaac Newton.   We did it
because we knew he could speak English.   While
we use the heavenly tongue, for the most part,
yet we have to learn it; and those of us who have
been here but a little while, and some to whom
languages come hard, often fall back upon our
native tongue.   And when we speak about our
former homes upon the earth, there are so many
things that have no counterpart in heaven, that
they can be spoken of in celestial language only
by borrowing terms from earthly tongues.

We found that the greatest of natural philosophers had taken the time, since he came here,
for studying many things that he had no time
for in England.   He had, moreover, been engaged in making the calculations needful for the
erection of new spheres to accommodate the increasing population of the heavenly system.   Yet
was he always at leisure to be spoken with; and

he conversed with us briefly upon the point of
our inquiry :

"That all beneficent service in the Land of
Shadow is but a struggle with adverse circumstances, is well illustrated by facts familiar to
me. My own discoveries were long rejected by
the schools. Yet I had no such trials to undergo
as did Copernicus, Galileo, and Kepler. The
Land of Shadow always stoned its prophets. As
God waited patiently for the disclosure of the
secrets of nature, so his instruments for making
the disclosures known were long rejected of men.
Printing was thought at first to be the work of
the devil: and when it was found to be a good
thing, a plan was made to monopolize it; which
was averted by a war, which scattered the print-
ers, and spread the art over Europe. When
Harvey issued a book upon the circulation of the
blood, his medical practice fell off at once, and
men said that he was insane. The introduction
of Peruvian bark as a medicine was at first
esteemed by Protestants as a wicked device of
the Jesuits. George Stephenson was regarded as
a lunatic for prophesying the advent of steam
locomotives. Under the reign of Edward I., a
man was executed for burning coal, 'a noxious
fuel' not legal to burn. And Philadelphia threw
brick-bats at the colliers, who lived by 'burning
stones.' "

II

At this point, we saw approaching us one whom our guest recognized as Bunyan; the friend of all pilgrims who come to this land. With him was a stranger, who had come to heaven from some far-off planet when a child; and he wondered much, when told of the difficulties of acquiring and imparting knowledge upon the earth.

A conversation now ensued, which illustrated other phases of the adverse circumstances which beset intellectual development, and the acquisition of knowledge, in the Land of Shadow. It related to the failure of cherished plans, and the inconveniences of sickness, and poverty. The adversities we had all undergone, greatly interested and surprised the youth who had come with the Pilgrim's Friend, as the Dreamer is called.

"Through imperfect knowledge," it was remarked by our guest, "aspiring men upon the earth, reach after unattainable ideals; they love that which is great and noble and inspiring,— and fail of their ambition. Yet that life is no failure, which is filled with high aiming, and desire for exalted service. It is by this means that the human mind is prepared for the opportunities of our heavenly life."

At this moment Blaise Pascal came, in search of our guest; and they went away in a few moments;—not however without a word from Pascal upon the topic we had been conversing about:

"In all our life in the Land of Shadow, we found one rule that would solve most questions of duty, and all questions of sorrow: it was, to consider life as a sacrifice, and that the accidents of life make no impression on the Christian mind, but as they interrupt or carry on that sacrifice."

It was the mission of Bunyan at our camp-fire, to disperse our group, and change our service. And in accordance with his directions, I removed to new quarters.

CHAPTER FOURTH

I

My new camp-fire, in other company, was kindled on the coast, at Rivermouth, where the River of Life flows into the sea. The spheres occupied as realms of the blessed are roomily built, so there is no crowding; and it is easy for every one to find place and time to be alone with God. That sorrow which is sometimes symbolized by the sea, finds no place upon the spheres that constitute the home of the angels of God.

Yet it came to me while I lived in the Land of Shadow, that the River of Life, alluded to in the Revelation, implied a water distribution analogous to that on the earth. Our Lord is the God of order and not of confusion; and in respect to the physical appearance of the spheres occupied by the people of God in world without end, there is much that is home-like. Nature has firm foothold in realms supernatural, furnishing those material worlds which localize heaven.

I found myself among people who had been

poor in the Land of Shadow, many of them from
the great cities; and there were others who had
been in very moderate circumstances; and some
there were who had been well-to-do in worldly
goods, and whose lives had been given to works
of charity. They were all of that happy class
who have a taste for country life. And here
each one had room enough. Some chose to
live in little neighborhoods, villages, or small
towns. And there were pleasantly located places
of social gatherings, — for diversion, for study,
and for worship.

Many of these people I had known before
coming here; and some were of my own kin. It
was a relatively new colony, the most having
been here but a short time. My duty and delight it was to go about among them, from house
to house, and to meet them at their gatherings;
and then, from time to time, bring to them
those from other localities who could best in-
struct them in that which they most needed to
learn.

I was still within sight of snow-clad mountains, and there were vast forest lands easily accessible; and there was much diversity of surface
towards the foot-hills of the great range. And
swift streams were running from the heights,
crossing the broad plains and intervale lands, and
then reaching the river not far from the point

where it joined the sea. I have been told that the apostles of our Lord who had been brought up near the Galilean sea, resided for some time near the mouth of this great river, when they first entered this mansion of our Father's house.

II

In one of the first houses I entered, I found a young man who once went to school to me. How well I remember his long sickness, not acute but protracted, months and years of wasting pain; and how patient he was, always looking for the light of God. He had a slight talent for versification, but gave to it no more pretentious name; it being with him but one form of rhetorical practice,—yet it well expressed the mood of the hour. Calling upon him the morning after he first knew from the physician that his earthly days were numbered, I found that he had whiled away the early hours in noting these lines:

> Thy gleaming wings,
> O Dove divine, from out the eastern skies,
> Attract my eyes;
> Thou art the dawn to break my gloom,—
> Thy glory brings
> To lowly room

The day, before the day begins.
With sickness sore, and grievous sins,
My night is weary till I see
The light celestial shine in Thee,—
Illumined wings to comfort me ;
Thou emblem art of peace,—
My mourning can but cease.

This was in the spring-time.   Upon his birthday in the early summer, he wrote :

THE MONTHS OF GOD

My earthly times are in Thy hands ;
My moments fall like sinking sands,
The glass soon runs its hourly course,—
My spirit flies to God its source.

My numbered months are all with Thee ;
The autumn winds may find me free,
In winter days my race may cease,—
Whate'er the time I am at peace.

No hap can ever fall to me, .
My life and years are marked by Thee ;
I joy in death as if my birth,—
My life above is nobler worth.

My natal day is in Thy hands,—
Farewell the earth, its seas and lands ;
My birthday comes, eternal joy,—
The perfect years, without alloy.

Here I found him now, surrounded by those dearest to him; and he was eagerly carrying on those pursuits which sickness and death had interrupted on the earth.

"My next neighbor," he said, "is George Herbert, who is still at work upon his quaint poesy. About half his time he dwells in the city; sometimes in one town, again in another. This, indeed, is his home; while the cities are his resorts for study or service. Here he lives in quiet content, with simple desires and thankful heart, and with leisure for delightful studies. To all newcomers he is a very patriarch in wisdom; and his going in and out among these homes is like that of a ministering angel. His golden crown is rarely seen even by his intimates, but his crown of spiritual wisdom is recognized by every one who meets him. And here he sings:

> "I seek not every star,
>   Nor wander near nor far:
>   My God is ever here,
>   My heart His gracious temple is;
>   My voice is ringing clear,
>   Since He is mine, and I am His."

CHAPTER FIFTH

ERELONG I went to another sphere in our Father's house. This was peopled for the most part by kindreds, tribes, and tongues from a part of the material universe far from the earth. To these, too, the Lord Jesus is the Great Shepherd: "Other sheep I have, not of this fold." They all speak one language, the heavenly. Yet there I found many of our earth-born angels, who had gone thither to learn arts and sciences and languages new to them; and to learn the gracious disposition of those peoples whose life experience had been so different from their own,—and in whose worlds afar there had never been either sin or disease or death. And I found him, of whom I was in search, discoursing to a great company concerning the sicknesses of the Land of Shadow, and the valley of the shadow of death :—

"The frail life of the night-moth, or the sun-lighted butterfly, is an emblem of human existence. We never could go into a company without noticing the garbs of mourning. The path of

life on the earth is beset by thorns, and rough with
graves.   There is no moment when there is not
mournful dirge-like music in the air.   And there
is an unending procession, with solemn tread,
moving towards the cemetery.   Any day, you may
observe the bereaved walking in the burial-ground,
listening for voices where there are none ; and
with dropping eyes searching for familiar faces
in the dust.   The air of the church-yard is filled
with bitter agony and strong crying ; moaning is
heard in the stillest day ; and in the brightest
sunshine there are always tears falling.

"Our most rapidly growing cities are girt
about by expanding and thickly peopled suburbs
of the dead.   As to mere number, our vast ware-
houses and roomy palaces are soon surpassed by
the pinched-up dwellings of our late merchants
and manufacturers.   The triumphant growth of
these rival cities of the dead would be more apparent, were it not that those still living require
so much wall and roof space to keep their persons from the weather, and so much massive
masonry for making, housing, or distributing
their goods ; while, upon the other hand, we
provide scanty dwelling room to the dead,—
packing their cast-off fleshly frame and raiment
in narrow compass, as we pack clothing in cedar
chests of little magnitude.   Otherwise, the multitude of small-sized cities of the dead, which

gird about our municipalities on every side, would crowd out the living, driving them to people new wildernesses. The advancing tombs would trench upon our business streets, and the unnumbered armies of the dead would quarter themselves in our homes. So that, for a monitory motto, there is no inscription more befitting the gateway of the cemetery than this : 'As a rival city, this will at last be triumphant.'

"Nor need you wonder, if those upon the earth, who are weary of their anguish, long to go home. Does not the music of the heavenly country find an echo in the hearts of the children of God, even in the Land of Shadow? Does not the life from above reinforce the dying life below, till pallid faces are transfigured by the uncreated Light ? So God comes to a man full of beneficent plans for holy service, and he takes the workman to himself, instead of accepting the work that he intended to do.

Book II

OUR FATHER'S HAND

CHAPTER FIRST

In the service at Rivermouth, I remained for a long time. After this, it was permitted me to carry out a plan that I have cherished ever since I was a little child. I never had time to be even ordinarily social; my kinsfolk, even of my own domestic circle, and many valued acquaintances, I had seen very little of, in my anxious care to work while the day lasted. Now I determined to take a little time to sit down and converse with kindred spirits, and not to feel hurried in it. I cannot tell now, how long it was; but the time flew very swiftly upon the wings of love, since these friends are so dear to me. Aside from those at Rivermouth, there were many in the Lake District; and some in the City of God, as we call that locality where there is no need of the light of the sun.

I

It was a great delight to me to have at last a little leisure for educating my eye and my hand.

I did some mechanical work in building and
decorating; having long been an expert in the
misuse of tools. The service I performed was
for a kinsman of mine, who had been a master
carpenter and excellent workman upon the
earth. He remarked that he was now occupied
with his books, and making up his education
which had been much neglected. He super-
vised my tool work, and I aided his studies.
Morning by morning, I heard him singing the
only hymn he ever composed :—

THE NEW DAY

Deep sorrow's night has passed away,
   The dawn of heaven is here ;
The face of Jesus makes new day,
   His light draws near.

All hail the Sun,—Thy glorious light
   Dispels the gloom of sin ;
My soul reflects the glory bright,
   Thy gates within.

'Tis dawn of endless brightening hours,
   The life of love for aye ;
New songs I hear in noontide bowers,—
   'Tis joy to die.

The night is past, the morning glows,—
   My spirit freed from clay;
The light of God around me flows,—
   His love my day.

My friend's home was under a great crag upon the border of a picturesque lake. We had been friends from boyhood, but our courses of life had widely separated. He was a man of good understanding, and of much native force of character; yet circumstances had been much against him, as to his acquiring other knowledge than that of carpentry. In the genial light of heaven, he was developing intellectual aptitudes which I had never suspected in the Land of Shadow. And he had been during many years tried as gold is tried; and by this test it was found that in respect to sterling qualities of character he compared well with certain angels, who had never been tempted to curse God and die when overwhelmed by disaster.

He had been defrauded, and made to lose this world's goods by no fault of his own; and he had survived the members of his own household, who had been suddenly removed one after another; and then he had been smitten by a loathsome disease, under such circumstances that he suffered neglect,—and yet he bore it all like an angel before he entered into angelic company. When, however, I mentioned this circumstance, he said:—

"That was not so; for I was surrounded by the arms of Infinite Love, and was ministered unto by the angels of God. And I should have been indeed an ingrate, if by complaint I had disgraced and disheartened my wife and my son and my daughter, who in turn left the heavenly mansions to watch over me. Nor could I ever have been unmindful of the Divine love, and provident favor."

And now it appeared, that it was through his experiences of grief that he had been detached from his hard grip upon the things of earth. "It was," he said, "much as if our Father had taken me by the hand, and led me along in the dark, until I reached his own abode, where there is no need of the sun."

II

Crossing the lake, one evening at the approach of twilight, I came upon a great camp-fire, in a little opening between wide-spreading hemlocks, not far from the water, where the party was celebrating the heavenly birthday of a little child. The family circle was now complete. They were friends very dear to me upon the earth.

"In the month of January, every year," said the mother, "I used to bury over again my husband. 'Let not that day be joined unto the days of the year,' was my prayer. The weeks of sickness, the days of agonizing doubt, the hour

of dying, and the hour for closing the grave,—
they all came back to me. But when little Jamie
left me, to follow his father, I knew, then, that
God was determined to have my whole heart.
And after that, I set my face towards my Father's
house."

"Our heavenly birthdays," said the father, "we
always observe with glee; and we forget our earthly sorrows, as waters that have passed away."

"It is well," said Jamie's guardian angel, "for
the multitudinous children of sorrow to grieve
and moan. God does not expect them to be as
heartless as stones. They are to be troubled, they
are to be bowed down greatly, they are to go
mourning all the day long. It is, that their eyes
may look upward, that they may behold our Father's face,—the Infinite Pity. It is, that they
may feel about in the darkness to find our Father's hand,—that they may follow its leading.
He will lead them home at last."

"The upwelling and the falling of tears," I
said, "must be as important in the eyes of God,
and as much under his direction, as the rise and
fall of planets. He who notes the fall of the
sparrow, says, 'Not a tear shall fall to the ground
without your Father.'"

"Melodious is the music," the guardian angel
said, "that floats to us, far over the deep waters
of affliction."

And then we all went down to the lake shore, and joined our voices :—

> Praise ye the Father, God of love;
> Praise ye the Son, in heights above ;
> Praise ye the Spirit, Heavenly Dove :
> 　Blessed Trinity.

CHAPTER SECOND

I

ALL the twilight hours I floated on the lake, having for my companion Jamie's guardian angel. He told me of his care for the child in his cradle days in the Land of Shadow; and in these later days of heavenly life, until his mother's coming. And how he was commissioned by our Father to abide with this family until the children should come to maturity.

"I have lived in heaven for many ages," he said, "coming hither from the Nile. I was a Hebrew child, not rescued like Moses. And when I learned what my countrymen endured, I was glad to be spending peaceful years in the City of God, where the Presence angels care for the babes that come hither; and where I was trained as God's child. As I grew older, I was sent to follow the wanderings of the Israelites in the wilderness, that I might be helpful to little children. And it has been so beautiful a service, that I have, during all these centuries, chosen to minister to the babes of earth, rather than stay here to study, or to engage in other forms of service. It is said that our Lord has brought many sons unto glory; and it has been my happy lot to have brought a good many of them."

"You must very often," I said, "have had a harder time in dealing with the parents than the children."

"The greatest difficulty," he replied, "that I have experienced with older people in the Land of Shadow, is in respect to their unbelief. Perhaps it is not to be wondered at,—the way they have been brought up. They so far misapprehend the character of God as to imagine that he has prepared an unthinkable heaven. They fancy it to be a strange and abnormal state, in which spirits without any fixed habitation go floating about; or else a country of serious saints in white, all absorbed in worship,—in a highly artificial, made-up life."

"If it were possible," I said, "for people on earth to know of some connecting link between the seen and the unseen, they would feel differently about it."

"But do they not have the Word of God?" he asked. "It is written, that the men of Nineveh, and the queen of the earth, would be known in the future state; that the apostles would be known, and know each other as apostles; that Moses and Elijah knew each other, the one going to heaven five or six hundred years after the other; that Martha would know her brother after the resurrection; that apostles would know their converts in heaven; and that the martyrs would know each other in our Father's house. Nor is there, in the heavens above or the earth beneath, any reason why saints in heaven should be kept ignorant of each other. Do men so misjudge God, as to think that he would cast them into a barren, unsocial state, where former associations are utterly unknown, allowing them to be more ignorant in heaven than they were upon the earth? Why do they not reason, that if God gave his Son, he will also, with him, freely give all things?"

II

Approaching us upon the water, we saw a father and son,—the latter having but recently appeared from the Land of Shadows.

"If God," said the son, "had not led me by my father's death to think of the most important things in life, I should have wandered far from that which is noblest and best; and I thank God for all my earthly sorrow. It was the hymn that was sung at my father's funeral service that impressed my mind; I knew that it was so like him.

"SING ALLELUIA

" Do not weep as ye stand here,
  Hither came I without fear, Alleluia.

" Withered life is never mine,
  I am branch of heavenly Vine, Alleluia.

" Fruitless life I do not mourn,
  Branch from Vine was never torn, Alleluia.

" Life is hid with Christ in God,
  Death's deep vale the Christ hath trod, Alleluia.

" Clad in robes of life divine,
  I have reached the heavenly line, Alleluia.

" Sing, for joy of heart is mine;
  Sing, till joy of heart is thine,—Alleluia."

"This hymn," said the father, "was written
by my mother; and we sang it at the side of
her casket. It was so like her. When it came
time for her to die, she was glad. And it was
the cheerful view she took of dying, that turned
me away from pursuits that were not the best
for me. It was her precious memorial upon
earth, that the world was better for her life."

"It is the first lesson of sorrow," said the
guardian angel, "that those who are bereft, learn
to look upon their departed friends not as bodies, but as spirits."

"Yet," I replied, "their grief would be more readily assuaged, if they could understand the mystery of the spiritual body; and if they could know how real and substantial life is, in the Light of our Father's House."

"After all, however," the angel replied, "the assuaging of grief is not the most important thing; the most important thing is, that men so yield to the dispensation of God, as to be led by our Father's hand to our Father's house."

CHAPTER THIRD

I

THERE is no night in the system of spheres that constitute the home of the blessed from all parts of the universe. The night shineth as the day; there being no hour in which the sky is not brilliant with varied lights, electrical, and stellar, and from satellites that attend these spheres of God. The twilight hours, in which all work ceases, and all heaven is given to social enjoyment, or to solitary communion with him who maketh the night light round about us,—these are the hours in which heaven is self-conscious or thoughtful of its own bliss. It was in these twilight hours, that I conversed the most with friends where I was a guest.

One night, I set out alone to walk to the top of a mountain whose base was not far off; walking, in order that I might often pause by the way, in spiritual communion with him who made the mountains and the sea. And I planned to reach the top, in season to make notes of the pageantry of the clouds at sunrise.

All along the way, I could but think of the scenes transpiring every moment in the Land of Shadows. An old neighbor of mine came here three months ago; and now one sits alone :—

" An empty heart, with cries unstilled;
An empty house, with love unfilled:
These are the things our Father willed."

And ten weeks ago my cousin died, leaving her babe and her husband. He goes about the house now, crying,—

" Oh for the touch of a vanished hand,
And the sound of a voice that is still."

" To them all," I said, " the Land of Shadow is next door to the Land of Silence. Yet it is no permanent condition,—the souls of men soon leave it."

Just then, as I neared the topmost ridge, I heard a swift rustling sound; and I saw that a company of angels had touched the highest crags before me. Eye hath not seen, nor ear heard, neither hath entered into the heart of man, that which God hath laid up for those that love him. The higher forms of experience in the heavenly world, can be expressed only in untranslatable terms of the heavenly language. Nor can I find words to describe the beauty of these beings, their garments, their mien, and all that their

eyes were speaking. They were earth-born
angels who were just returning from a visit to
the Land of Shadow; some having never been
there till now, since leaving it ages ago. Some
of them were husbands and wives, parents and
children of far-away generations. Some had
been the founders of the Church of God in savage districts on the earth, or in other worlds.
From what was said, I imagined that their leader
was St. Paul, and that some at least were members of the apostolic churches.

There was in each face such mark of strong
individuality, after three or four score of scores
of years in heaven, that each one was free from
that sense of dependency on each other which
had been incidental to their early earthly experiences. They were now indeed the friends of
God, even more emphatically and peculiarly than
of each other. They bore the marks of being
allied to the Infinite Friendship; without those
expressions of countenance that indicate the
limitations of love, in earthly experience. Since
I reached the heavenly world, I had not till now
seen such majestic faces; there indeed were the
sons and daughters of the Almighty, so abiding
in his love, so filled with his desires and ani-
mated by his purposes, that, while they plainly
loved each other, yet for all spiritual kinship
they were allied to God as intimately as if

wedded friends. Some of them had reached high rank among the principalities and powers of worlds on high.

Discerning that I was, relatively, a stranger in a strange land, one approached me, and I was made to sit with them; and one tarried with me a little while, after the others had resumed their journey to another sphere.

II

"I can read your thoughts," he said. "You wonder how far domestic love survives the grave. Know, then, that friendship never dies, love lives on forever; yet the need of abiding stead-fastly in pairs, in this location or that, has gone by forever. The wife whose cares could not be laid aside, and who could never in all her years catch up with the routine of her daily service, has now the opportunity for varying her work. Her children are perhaps thousands of years old, and she and her husband but a trifle older; and the service of their Lord has given them diversi-fied employment here and there in the realms of the blessed, or among the abodes of the needy in other worlds. With many centuries of mental development, and increasing vigor of powers, both husband and wife have become less de-pendent on each other, and their relation to God has become more intimate. And in the on-sweeping cycles of life and love divine, the development of individual finite character leads every one forth into a life like that of the oldest angels, the career of Gabriel, the four-and-twenty elders, or the living creatures that are but conscious voices in rendering ceaseless homage to God Most High.

"The fires of animal instinct, and envy, and jealousy, never darken the sky in the spheres of endless felicity; and every part of our natures is strengthened, and our highest faculties are brought into play by intimacies formed on high. Nor is there in the heavenly world any ungracious personality, or one so absorbed in himself as to forget others; and good breeding and a nice appreciation of what is fitting is now the heritage of those who were relatively rude in the Land of Shadow. So that the opportunities for friendly acquaintance and intimate companionship are found on every side,—according to individual nature, tastes, acquirement, and accustomed duties. Yet in no age will the unselfish loves of earth—friendships formed in earthly fires, and the mutual helpfulness, and the experience of common joys and sorrows in the Land of Shadows—be forgotten in the spiritual sympathy and solace and light and love of our Father's house.

"Man on the earth has a physical basis. He is to train for God the children of immortality. The family life is the divinely appointed means for this. But man in heaven has a spiritual basis of life, a spiritual body; and there is neither marrying nor giving in marriage. These spheres rather are peopled by those who have left in the grave all that was earthly and sensual, all their weaknesses and infirmities. They are so purified from all grossness of nature, so sanctified by the Spirit, that they are spoken of as the Church of God, the Bride of the Heavenly Bridegroom.

"While, then, we are to look 'for it, that the family relation will continue in heaven, as long as it may be useful to the individuals composing it in giving love some finite object to lean upon for mutual support, yet, in the lapse of centuries, the love of every individual towards God will so expand with the increasing knowledge of his character, that every one will be drawn to him as the dearest Friend. And every finite soul in its development, and in becoming more like God, will feel less need of finite beings for mutual help; but the mind of each will be so fixed on God, that the metaphor of bridegroom and bride will best express the relation established between God and those who love him.

"This then is the meaning of what Jesus says,

that in heaven there shall be neither marrying
nor giving in marriage, but all shall be as the
angels of God."

III

With these words my companion departed;
and I swiftly returned to that home whose guest
I was.

Then I understood what had not been clear to
me before, that, in the sphere where I am now,
there are vast numbers of homes where the individual members of the domestic circle are best
helped spiritually by maintaining family relations
under more favorable conditions than the earth
afforded; but with the advance of every one in
years and experience, and the development of
capacity for enjoyment and service—in short,
with the unfolding of their godlike natures—they
enter into higher schools on other spheres, and
then they become more like the angels of God,
and in the progress of time there is less thought
about domestic life than was needful at a less
mature period.   Then will be fulfilled those
precious words of our Lord, that we shall be
equal unto the angels, and the children of
God.

Every house then among us is to-day like a
temple, and every hour is heard ascending the

voice of praise and thanksgiving to God. Our
love, our memory, our reason abide in realms of
light; and, having passed through the article of
death, they live on forever. And since our
characters are built up by love, we cling to those
whom we have so long loved and known,—in adversity, in desolation, in our burial of cherished
hopes, over coffin lids and little graves; and if,
in after-ages, the range of friendship is less lim-
ited, we shall still be always grateful for our
earthly, as for our heavenly home. And if we
cannot intimately know and love all alike, we
will walk hand in hand with our loved ones,—into
whose eyes we have looked for sunshine amid all
the darkness and tearfulness of the Land of
Shadows, — until that day when Christ is so
formed within us as to be not only the hope of
glory, but the present passion of the soul, the
all-absorbing life and love of the Heavenly Bridegroom.

Some indeed reach this state sooner than others, but our Lord is not the God of confusion,
but of order. The great change of the human
soul in passing from life to life is not so great as
to confound the spirit of him who enters into
life everlasting. It is our Father's hand that
upholds us, when in the Land of deep Shadows
we stand by the grave of all earthly hope and
love; and it is in his companionship that we are

led across that wide-stretching desert, which we had expected to tread alone ; and he leads us, in earthly bereavement, to become more acquainted with him, to lean upon him, with whom we shall walk for ages unending.

CHAPTER FOURTH

WHAT could be more wearying to the child of heaven than ceaseless sunlight, or the sight of the same flowers upon the same stem ? The orderly succession of seasons contributes much to the felicity of existence; and it is easy to go hither and thither, or from world to world at will. In the most enchanting season is observed that crown of days, our Children's Festival. It is a reunion of all parents and children who have been reunited since the festival day preceding.

Then it is that multitudes whom no man can number from all our heavenly spheres flock hither. They come, all those children who went to heaven as babes, and never knew an earthly home; they come, the sons of God from all those parts of the universe in which there is no sin nor death; they come, those guardian spirits whose love and sympathy have been poured out for years, in the care of some earthly home; they come, who are glad of heart over sinners repenting,—they come to hear the story of those whom our Father's Overshadowing Hand has led by bereavement away from the Land of Shadows, to plant their feet within the threshold of eternal life.

I

With the thronging multitudes I went, thinking to find some that were personally known to me. There was A., I said, who used to be in my Sunday-school class. She was endowed with one of those happy, sunny, singing dispositions which is an unceasing benediction to the home which shelters it. She belonged, too, to that great class of people whose physical condition is such as to transmit disease to their children, whose stay upon the earth must be brief; they being really the parents of angels, rather than of those who are to dwell long upon the earth. Their anxieties, watchings, and affections are expended upon the children of our Father's house, who are soon called home.

> "Sweet the lives
> That glide away without the sense of ills."

Infants die; the moment they come into life, they fly from it, to their home in heaven. They are called into being, touching the earth; and parental love is fastened to them, and they depart, drawing after them the threads of love that are to be henceforth fastened on the unseen. A. was so bowed down by her child's death, that she felt that she could never sing again. Yet one Sunday she told me that near the end of the morning service, it seemed as if something had lightened her heart, and that now she must sing for gladness. New life had come to her from the death of her babe. And so effectively had the cords of her mother-love been fastened to the unseen that, afterwards, she always told me that it seemed as if her little one was beckoning to her. And this morning I met her, with her babe in her arms.

"My life," she said, "was like a voiceless reed. It needed to be pierced, to make it melodious."

II

Then there was B., whose public work was carried on for years, with constantly recurring visions of domestic tragedy,—a dying child, or the cold clay, invading the class-room. One after another, his children remained to him only as visions and memories.

"Our children," he said to me, "are of use mainly, to discipline their parents; a discipline perfected by the most dreadful of tragedies."

Yet the promise of our Lord, "I go to pre-

6

pare a place for you," was to him fulfilled by the preparation of his own heart for the place, and of the place for his heart, by the dwelling of his children in the unseen world.

And now this morning his children have come running to me in great joy, — "Father has come." And they led me to him.

III

Then there was my old neighbor, C., far down the river on which I was born; she was of my own kin. I saw her to-day, with her children; one of whom had been cut down in battle, one without warning when at school, and one by lingering painful disease at home.

"I feel assured," she told me long ago, "that what gives me grief, gives my loved ones the greatest joy. And for myself, when it is dark, to whom can I go but to my Father?

"'My Father, it is dark.' 'Child, take my hand,
  Cling close to me; I'll lead thee through the land.'

"My trial has led me straight into the arms of my Saviour."

IV

And here too I find D., whom I knew so well when a school-girl in England. She knew, in her domestic life, every winding in the vale of tears. Her face was changed through sorrows. The laughter which had lurked under her eye-lids and about her red lips had died out. Her physical beauty had been laid in her child's grave; and the color had gone from her life to the flowers which touched them, before they were left to fade upon the precious mound. Her summer days were spent in gathering floral offerings to decorate the realm of death.

"I give you joy, my darling," she said, when her second child joined the first.

"I am glad he has gone to keep Winnie company," she wrote me. "And yet, now that the grave is covered, I constantly hear his foot-fall on the stair; and his voice is lingering in the house. I waken in the night at his call, and I break my heart all day at the emptiness of the rooms where I go mechanically to find him. Nor can I set to rights the desolated apartment where he died, nor ever fold his deserted garments, nor set to rights my own bleeding heart, nor pack away my love with his clothing."

Yet she did set heart and house to rights;

and she went out into the byways and gave to God all the time she had once given to her babes,—in caring for the waifs who know no mother's love.

"And now I am glad," she said, when I met her, "that God privileged me in having to do with the beginning of immortality for my children. They drew me away from myself; they developed in me an unselfish love; they led me to God. And their training in our Father's house has been better than I could have given them. It was, indeed, beautiful that I had anything earthly so precious to give to my Saviour as my sweet babes."

V

"'What I do, thou knowest not now, but thou shalt know hereafter,'" were the words of him who presided at this service. "We did not know in the Land of Shadow what was meant by the mystery of suffering which we endured, but we yielded ourselves joyfully to the hand of our Father, to be led by him in his own way to the Light of our Father's House; and now we thank God for all the way in which he led us. Deep and dark was our night of sorrow, but joy cometh in the morning.

"And now all the parents and children who have been reunited since our last Festival, will sing 'Home at Last.'"

Rank upon rank, rose the millions upon millions, in the great amphitheatre of the mountains; and their voices were like the sound of many waters :—

"On the jasper threshold standing,
  Like a pilgrim safely landing,
  See the strange bright scene expanding!
      Ah, 'tis heaven at last!

"What a city! what a glory!
  Far beyond the brightest story
  Of the ages old and hoary;
      Ah, 'tis heaven at last!

"Softest voices, silver pealing,
  Freshest fragrance, spirit-healing,
  Happy hymns around us stealing,
      Ah, 'tis heaven at last !

"Gone the vanity and folly,
  Gone the dark and melancholy,
  Come the joyous and the holy;
      Ah, 'tis heaven at last !

"Not a tear-drop ever falleth,
  Not a pleasure ever palleth,
  Song to song forever calleth;
      Ah, 'tis heaven at last !

"Christ himself the living splendor,
Christ the sunlight mild and tender;
Praises to the Lamb we render;
Ah, 'tis heaven at last!"

And then they chanted the Thanksgiving and
Commemoration for the Babes: as it was written
by that sainted woman who rendered earthly
praise to our Heavenly Father for his care of
her five little ones, who were led before her into
the Light of our Father's House:

"Lord, thou hast let thy little ones depart in peace.

"Lord Jesus, thou hast received their spirits, and hast
opened unto them the gates of everlasting glory.

"Thy loving Spirit leads them forth into the land of
righteousness, into thy holy hill, into thy heavenly kingdom.

"Thou didst send thine angel to meet them, and to carry them into Abraham's bosom.

"Thou hast placed them in the habitation of light and
peace—of joy and gladness.

"Thou hast received them into the arms of thy mercy,
and given them an inheritance with thy saints in light.

"There they reign with thine elect angels and thy
blessed saints departed, thy holy prophets and glorious
apostles, in all joy, glory, felicity and blessedness, for
ever and ever.   Amen."

CHAPTER FIFTH

FROM the festival I went home with an old sailor whom I used to know. He had had hard fortune in the Land of Shadow, and never knew what a home was till now. It was built upon a high headland overlooking the sea. And as we sat there night after night by our twilight camp-fire he detailed to me with great minuteness how he came to know God, as he called it.

"The most of the trouble was," he said, "that I misapprehended God. I distrusted God, in-stead of distrusting my apprehensions of him, which were the real mistake. I grieved over the ways of God, because I was ignorant of them. When I knew better, I rejoiced every hour.

"By his rod and his staff he comforted me. It was by the rod of correction; and he com-forted me through blessed sorrows. It is no matter whether he comes with a rod or with a crown, if he only comes himself; so Samuel Rutherford tells me.

"It was when I was forty years old, that I set out to untie my heart from all earthly things, and to tie it to God only. And after that, the consolation of the Gospel gave me serenity of spirit."

And then he insisted upon my learning one of his sea-songs, that his chaplain wrote when he was a man-of-war's man :—

THE OUTWARD BOUND

The sky, the sky, above, below,—
The stars astream in swift onflow ;
The earth is lost, I'm outward bound,—
The shores of earth no more are found.

Eternal years are mine to sail
Through realms afar with favoring gale ;
The singing spheres, O blissful sound,—
I sail the sky, I'm outward bound.

The sparkling suns, the glancing rays,
The shining nights, the dancing days ;
The waves' unrest my firmest ground,—
Hurrah, hurrah ! I'm outward bound.

I hail, I hail that beacon star
Whose glow illumes the waves afar;
I'm borne by streams beyond control,
O homeward bound art thou my soul.

The free, the free, I sail the sea,
The waves that bear me home to Thee,
Thou Beacon Light of every world ;
I reach the goal, my sails are furled.

THE LIGHT OF OUR FATHER'S HOUSE

CHAPTER FIRST

THE time had now come in which I was to abide for a season in the City of God, as it is set forth in the visions of Patmos. Not that God is there in any sense which localizes the First Cause of all things ; not that God is there, in any sense in which he is not also in every part of the heavenly spheres, and in every part of the material universe.

The peculiar glory and splendor of the city, as it is expressed in symbol by the Revelator, is but a type of that which exists in every part of the blissful spheres of heaven. And the light of God is so displayed, that there are no shadows falling,—nor are there twilight hours.

Here is observed that Marriage Supper of the Lamb of God, which symbolizes the intimate relation between the Infinite and the finite,—the friendship of God, and the love and adoration of his people.

Hither come all the angels of God on great festal days ; for worship, and holy convocation. Here are the great treasure - houses of

celestial wisdom, and of knowledge pertaining
to all worlds.   Here are the facilities for acquiring that intellectual and moral equipment by
which a child of earth may bear his part with
honor among the principalities and powers of
the heavenly world ; and here he is fitted to become an instrument for carrying out the purposes of the Infinite Majesty in conducting the
affairs of the universe.

Those who are to reign as kings and priests
unto God are here in training for their high
station, that they may be prepared to image
forth the wisdom of God and all his holy attributes ; that they may be of service to him in
making known the love of God, and his holy
character, wherever there are moral beings made
in his image.

He who works by general laws, and by secondary causes, in the creation and development of
the material universe, conducts in like manner
his moral government in all worlds.   And here
in the City of God are those great schools in
which those elect spirits,—whom we so sadly
missed when they were removed from the Land
of Shadow, those chosen of God from the foundation of the world to be of service to him in
the conduct of his moral government,—are in
training for their service.

Hither come from all celestial spheres those

mighty angels, who have been, during imme-
morial ages, the honored instruments of the Ancient of Days.   And the ceaseless unfolding of
the purposes of the Infinite God is always in-
volving new plans to be executed.   The changing aspects of the material creation, the rise and
fall of new worlds, the kindling of the fires of
the sun, the development of life upon cooling
globes, the establishment of those who are moral-
ly like God in every habitable world to bear sway
as his children, the care of the nations, the moral
education of men in every sphere,—these are
the works which the First Cause of all things
commits to secondary instruments so far as they
may be fitted to execute them.

It is this which arouses every faculty of those
spirits who are ambitious to search out the mysteries of the universe,—to know how to perform
the works of God after him.   And the Infinite
wisdom and power are so imparted to those beings made in his image, that in the progress of
ages, there will be principalities and powers in
worlds on high well fitted to act as the instruments of God.

It is in this sense that God is peculiarly manifested in the city called by his name.   With all
material splendors, all that eye can wish or heart
conceive ; with unceasing adoration of the Infinite Power ; with the immediate presence of

the Father, and the Son, and the Holy Spirit, as
manifest in the Son of Man, the Son of God, the
Lamb slain from the foundation of the world,
the expression of Infinite Love to finite beings
made in their measure like himself in mental
constitution and moral attributes;—besides all
this, there is all that is requisite for reaching an
intellectual apprehension of the unfolding purpose of the Almighty, which was, and is, and is
to come,—and an intellectual and moral fitness
to serve Him who hath made all things, and
without whom nothing is made that is made.

CHAPTER SECOND

I

Upon this particular occasion of my entering into the City, where I had been so often for a day, the first person I met was my old college president; Greylock, as we loved to call him, from the mountain near his door.

"What could have been more certainly anticipated than this," he said. "He who made the world of insect life, also made the higher forms of animals,—and man as the crown of earth. Then having developed in man those powers which are but little lower than angelic, he has prepared this world for the further unfolding his godlike nature under favoring conditions. What, indeed, could have been more certainly anticipated than that he who made earth, should have made heaven. When the First Cause of all things mapped out his work in creation, he not only provided for insects, animals, and man, but he prepared a system of spheres where no sin might enter, where those beings from the Land of Shadow who are of the highest moral aspiration, may come at some future time to share the thrones of intellectual and moral supremacy in carrying out the designs of the Creator. This system of things is as solidly based as old Greylock."

II

I went into one of the schools for young children. There are not fewer than twenty to twenty-five millions of infants who are under two years old, brought here from out the Land of Shadow every year, who will scarce remember that they ever had any other home than heaven. Their care requires a vast organization of teachers; and I met a good many who were trained in the normal schools of my native State.

When I began to teach, I lived in the family of an aged pastor with long white locks, and a sweet affability, a dignified and courteous bearing, who gave an incredible amount of time to recording the weather three times a day during seventy years, and who was, too, a painstaking local historian writing down in a clear copperplate hand the details of domestic life in a few scores of families. I found him here, devoting himself to beloved service, in recording the distribution of a certain grade of pupils throughout the continents of this primary sphere.

I went into the map-and-globe room, to examine the aspect of the various worlds in this system of heavenly orbs. I did this, I confess, to reassure myself, since all that I had seen in this land seemed to me like a waking dream; so beautiful, indeed, as to be like enchantment.

"God dwells in light," said the teacher to her class of little ones. "It is a definite place, where he manifests his peculiar glory. This is the place, to which Christ's body came on his ascension. This is the place, where the glorified bodies of Enoch and Elijah are now. This is the place, where the spiritual body of the great Law-giver of Israel now abides, just as he was seen by the disciples in the vision of Transfiguration. This is that better country, for which Abraham looked,—solid and substantial as Canaan. This is the city which hath foundation. This is the house not made with hands, eternal in the heavens."

"And here, my precious children," she said, after first, as I thought, wiping away the tears that welled to her eyelids, "here is a globe that shows you how it looks in the Land of Shadows. This is where you were born, in North China. The earth fled like a dream from your eyes, when you were but babes; and you awakened to taste the eternal fountains of the water of life, in the Light of our Father's House."

7

And afterwards she told me that she had been a missionary in North China, and that she had no sooner learned the language than she was called here.

"Four or five millions of little babes come here every year from China," she said; "and when I came here, there were too few helpers to care for them. It is true that the climate there was unfavorable to me, but it was also true that there was a work for me here; since I understood well the circumstances in which these children were born, and how to adapt the truth to their minds, and I knew the language which some of them were beginning to talk or understand."

III

It now appeared that this teacher had been once under my parochial care; but she had so changed since then, that I did not know who it was. And she brought to me her own child, whose body had been laid beside hers, in what had seemed to me that far-off mission land.

"'Neither can they die any more, for they are equal unto the angels.' This," she said, "is a very precious text to me. And I am very happy in my work. The minds of these children here develop naturally, like flower and fruit from good seed, under genial conditions, without blight or imperfection or taint of anything that is evil. They will certainly walk worthy of their new names, which are written in the Book of Life."

And after a moment's pause, she added : " It was very much to me, in coming here, where I felt almost like a stranger, to be able at once to exercise confidence in all whom I met at the first. It is very beautiful to live where there is no sin. And I can see, too, that the conditions here are so favorable for mental development, that I shall be quite willing to have another take my place, that I may get more time for my own studies. My little boy has become so mature and manly now, that we are soon going out into the country, where I can command my time better ; and where the opportunities for the kind of work I wish to do, are superior to anything offered here."

CHAPTER THIRD

I

NOT far from the tree of life, in the midst of the Paradise of God, I encountered a group, conversing among themselves; and they asked me to be of their number.

"This is certainly a better country for the pursuit of systematic courses of study, than the Land of Shadow," said one. "For months together I used to be all broken up, first by one grief, and then by another. It is the absence of sorrow that strikes me as the strangest thing in this country. I used to sit, and sing,—

> " 'Jerusalem, my happy home,
> Name ever dear to me,
> When shall my labors have an end
> In joy and peace in thee?
> Oh when thou city of my God
> Shall I thy courts ascend?'

And now that I am safely here, I am too full of content to sing at all. I praise God in silence;

and he knows how my heart is overflowing in love and thanksgiving."

"Neither shall there be any more pain," responded one who sat near him, "for the former things are passed away; that we may be all presented faultless before the presence of His glory."

"Was it not written," said another, "that we should have a body like unto the glorious body of our Lord? The spiritual body can have no infirmity, and the inhabitants shall not say, I am sick. I find in the heavenly language no words to express what we mean by burning fever, tainted air, sudden accident, age, or death."

"I cannot quite understand it," remarked his brother, next to him, who had just come from the Land of Shadows, "nor can I make up my mind that my head will ache no more, that my eyes will cease from tears, and my lips utter no grief, nor my hands be weary, nor my feet tire."

"I was born blind," another said, "and I never saw the earth. I first open my eyes on heaven, as if I had been born in this country. I think of the earth as the Land of Blackness; here it is all Light, the Light of God gladdening my eyes and heart."

And then I said,—"The bier and the pall are not borne through these streets; no grave is opened here; and no one hears the wail of mourners.   But I have found the word 'tears' in the heavenly language; and it is said that 'God shall wipe away all tears.'"

I had not observed one who had come, and who stood behind me.   I heard his voice:—

"I find that my memory of rock and flame do not disturb my heavenly holiday."

"I am glad," said a stout-framed man, directly in front of me, "to be rid of disordered nerves, and the sins which plant their roots in the nervous system."

"I am glad," said his comrade, "that it is right for me to do just what I want to, in this country; for here I always want to do what is right."

And then I saw coming into our company, one whom I had last seen as an aged and decrepit woman, who lived on the bank of the Connecticut.   And the last time I called upon her, she had said, that there being no more sorrow, and that God would wipe away all tears, meant more to her than the walls of jasper; and that the idea of rest was so fixed in her mind, that she wished to sleep a thousand years.   And now she was singing like a child in immortal youth:—

"The ransomed of the Lord shall come to Zion with songs, and everlasting joy upon their heads; they shall obtain joy and gladness, and sorrow and sighing shall flee away."

Just then, I heard a chorus of sweet voices approaching, singing :—

Thou strangely sobbing sea
Of earth, thy voice is never heard on high :
Thy moaning waves in caverns sleep ;
Thy tempests loud in silence deep
Are chained ; nor stormy breath nor heaving sigh
Is heard from sorrow's sea.

O surging, grieving sea,
Be still, in all thy wild and restless waves :
Thy deep no more shall call to deep ;
O'er thee no more shall widows weep :
Sweet songs arise from all thy wrecks and graves,
O changing, tuneful sea.

We sing thy songs, O sea :
No more thy parting tide on earth shall roll ;
The heavens are new, and new the sea,—
All earthly griefs and shadows flee.
Thy voice in many waters, free from dole,
Now raise to God, O sea.

II

Then in a moment there came along a company of slaves from the West Indies, led by a Moravian missionary, who had upon his own request been sold as a slave that he might tell them about Jesus Christ. They had almost forgotten that they had ever been in such low estate.

Wearing crowns of gold and walking the golden streets, they had no need for labor, to supply any needs of the spiritual body. They hunger no more, neither thirst any more; neither do they labor, nor are they weary. The servant is free from his master; nor can it be told whether he be not a governor or king in the New Jerusalem.

"'Jerusalem that is above is free, which is the mother of us all,'" said their leader. "Death knocked off our fetters, and we are captives no more. Our galled shoulders, weary with earthly burdens, now wear imperial robes. Our warfare has given place to triumph; our darkness to day.

"And we find that this freedom from cramping cares, is favorable to our pursuit of knowledge. All the patience and skill we learned below is of use above. And the narrow and strait gate we entered, has opened for us into infinite breadth and height of life, and the slaves of earth find themselves at liberty to enter into all paths of heavenly wisdom. We find twelve manner of fruits upon the tree of life, and we can make our choice."

III

Then I saw a long procession of pilgrims from the Land of Shadow, who had just come

in, under a convoy of angels; and they were
singing :—

"Dear heavenly home!
This morn, our souls have reached thy peaceful shore;
We've won the crown of life, to sin no more.
Banish'd all doubt and fear forever more,
    To reign with Christ above."

As one after another was met and drawn apart
by some of his kin or acquaintance, who thronged
the sides of the street, it was easy to learn the
stories of their varied lives.   Here was one who
never had a home, amid many places called home.

"O wanderer in life's desert, hither come," it
was said to him.   "Here thou shalt be abun-
dantly satisfied with the fatness of thy Father's
house; and thou shalt drink of the River of
Peace.   Blessed are the homesick, who come at
last to their home in glory.   For it is written,
that there remaineth a rest for the children of
God; a rest from cares, from fears, from foes,
from temptation, from sin.   'The road is short,
the rest is long.'   For this thy soul hath waited,
as they who watch for the morning; and now it
is morning."

Here came soldiers and sailors from distant
peril; and merchant adventurers, and travellers
from all lands.   A great number had been re-
leased from hospitals; or from earth's prison-

houses.   Some were from the spice islands, and
groves of palm ; others from arctic snows.   Here
were senators and statesmen, and very learned
men ; all had come, that they might now sit at
the feet of Jesus, and learn of him.   Here was
a mother, and a babe in her arms ; and many
mothers encircled them in sweet caresses.

And then I saw that the Son of Man, too, had
come, to welcome them all to his Father's house.

CHAPTER FOURTH

I

MY brother and I went forth one day soon after this, to explore this City, and see what it is like. It lieth four-square, and the height is equal to its length or its breadth. Or, if not literally so, yet the mountain summits within the city walls are of such altitude as to readily suggest the comparison alluded to by the Revelator.

"We can but think," said my brother, "that the Builder and Maker of this City has room enough in the universe to house his children without crowding."

"Then, too," I said, "it is plain that he who planted our first parents in a paradise, loves beauty."

Along the vales of waving palms, by the dancing waves of rippling rivers, or past the shining temples on the heights, among the groves, and by the sparkling fountains, we wandered. Many were the gates of pearl we saw ; they were always open, inviting us to hospitable entertainment in grounds and mansions where we caught glimpses

of white-robed throngs coming and going upon
some private festal occasion. Life-giving were
the leaves we plucked, and greatly we desired to
send them forth, for the healing of all nations.
And here and there, we rose to great heights of
green or jagged mountains; far up whose shadow-
less sides, rising in no light of the sun, we found
that architecture which indicates the perpetual
presence of the Lamb of God as the temple of his
people. And there in the ceaseless day, we could
but raise our triumphal songs. And there, upon
these Pisgah crags we could but bless that bright
moment, that sudden moment, that unexpect-
ed moment, when my brother was called from
out the Land of Shadows, and when his feet
were planted securely within the City of our
God.

"I had hoped, my brother, that you would
come soon," I said; "and I have, as our Master
directed, been preparing for you this dwelling-
place."

We could see, far away, the blue of the sea;
and the great River of Peace flowing through
fields of living green towards its ocean bed. Far
away stretched the fertile plains with their
growths of many-colored beauty. And far away,
on every side, we could see the many mansions
of our Father's house.

And then we went into the garden near the

house, and sat down by the stream, and listened to the waterfall ; and we dreamed of heaven.

"Can it be true, that we are here, at last ?"

And we dreamed of the Land of Shadows ; and we could but imitate the intercession of our Saviour, who ever liveth to plead for his Church upon earth,—and we greatly desired, for all our dear ones, that they should lay hold upon the precious promise made to them, of an inheritance incorruptible, undefiled, and that fadeth not away.

"I can understand now," my brother said, "that God has a certain type in world-making ; and that the material universe, of which the earth is one planet, is really built upon the pattern of the heavenly system of blessed spheres. And it is written that he who overcometh shall inherit all things ; and I will be his God, and he shall be my son. This City belongs to us ; and we have 'a right' to the tree of life,—it belongs to us. And I see nothing that defileth. The moral sky is full of sunshine. The Lord shall be unto thee an everlasting light, and thy God thy glory.

"'How happy
The holy spirits who wander here,
'Mid flowers that never fade or fall.
Though mine were the gardens of earth and sea,
Though the stars themselves had flowers for me,—

One blossom of heaven out-blooms them all.
Go wing thy flight from star to star,
From world to luminous world as far
As the universe spreads its flaming wall;
Take all the pleasures of all the spheres,
And multiply each through endless years,—
One moment of heaven is worth them all.' "

Then we were for a long time silent, each dreaming his dream of this world of beauty which belongs to us, as we belong to God.

" My brother," I said, " we have come to this City to study. How favorable are the conditions for intellectual advancement."

" The unique scenery will certainly influence our characters," he replied, " much as you were once so greatly helped by earthly forests and mountains and seas."

II

And now we were joined by our father, and mother, and sister, who had just returned from long journeying upon other spheres. My father had been a blacksmith, with strong arm, and great heart, who had devoted himself to doing good to others. My mother, who had lived to be of great age, was a very hard-working woman; of much intellectual force, with slight opportunity for schooling or study, save what she gained by devotional reading and meditation. My sister had lived very many years in heaven, and knew so much more about it than the others, that she was practically the head of the house.

My father always kept the world astir, so far as he could do it; and he was rejoicing in physical powers unwearied, by which he was a match for anything he might wisely undertake.

"I could never do as I would, till now," mother said; "and I have been spending some years in testing my latent mental forces to see what I am equal to, and what I can do best. I had been but dimly conscious of a talent for music, for painting, for the mechanic arts, for poetic and prose composition. The most I brought here was a good deal of executive power, and self-devotement to God and his work. I was advised to take as many years as I cared to, for ascertaining what I might most wisely do,—then to decide."

My sister had greatly outstripped us all in development of faculties and in attainments; having been a hard student in this country, where everything conspires to favor the unfolding of that part of our natures in which we are most like God. She had gained a power of perception which seemed to me like the wisdom of an angel of light.

With a childhood friend, she had roamed far

and wide from world to world; the spiritual
body moving like the spirit, as quickly as an act
of the will.   In a flash, one is wherever he wills
to be; penetrating whatever is interpenetrated
by the cosmic ether.   That sphere which she
had latest visited, is peopled with the oldest angels, those most nearly approaching the begin-
ningless life of God.   How old, no one could tell.
They measured life by the rise and fall of systems of stars in the material creation.

The young man who sat upon the stone at
the tomb of Jesus, was hoary, with unimagina-
ble lapse of years, before the foundation of the
world.   In all these cycles of unnumbered years
he had been accumulating wisdom; and all av-
enues of holy activity had been open to him,
during ages multitudinous as the drops of water
in the sea.   And the time will never come when
he is not fresh in youth.

"Let us thank God then, and take courage,"
said my father, "if we but follow in the path
where angel feet have trodden; if we climb the
heights to-day, where they were on yesterday;
if to-morrow, we press on, to reach the point
where they are to-day.   There must come a day,
as countless ages advance, when there will be
relatively little difference between one finite
creature and another; except what is made by
different natural endowments, and different pur-

suits, and such slight difference of time for development as is suggested by the lapse of a few
finite years compared with ages unending.

"Yet, when time is no longer, when the material worlds fall like withered leaves, when the
fires of all stars perish, then our increasing
knowledge of God in parts of his ways will lead
us as never before to understand the fathomless
chasm that exists between the finite and the Infinite ; and then as never before, we shall find,
each for himself and for herself, that the friendship of God becomes the all-absorbing passion of
the soul,—and we shall cling to him, as bride to
Bridegroom."

8

CHAPTER FIFTH

I

HAVING now gone over in my own mind with much painstaking the essential conditions that exist in this land for the unfolding of godlike powers, and having learned something of the possibilities offered, I could not but go away alone to some unpeopled realm, there to commune with God, to tell him all that is in my heart, my earnest longings to be of use as his instrument, my desire to learn the best course to take, and to commit myself to his leading,— "Be thou, O God, the guide of my youth."

And I determined to forsake father and mother and sister and brother, and cleave to God only as my portion, my Friend.

This indeed might imply no separation of domestic friends, but a certain living apart in spirit, making God first and last and always the most intimate of friends, who knoweth me altogether and to whom I lay bare every fibre of my being, and by whom I have a consuming passion to be filled, that I may be energized by him, and informed by his wisdom, and be led forth to purpose and to do according to his mind only,— he being my dwelling-place to all generations.

How long a period passed in my lone abiding I cannot tell, being not alone.   Yet, thereby, my mind was fitted to make intelligent inquiry as to possible paths for study and service.

II

For the relatively brief terms of study we had proposed to take in this City, my father chose that which would fit him to be of quite immediate spiritual service to earthly mechanics, and my brother sought systematic courses for a score of years, while my mother and sister decided upon such work as would best serve them in seeking the advantages of another heavenly sphere.

For my part, I sought out my old college president, Greylock, and advised with him. His well-disciplined mind, his range of acquaintance, and his experience in the educational work of the City of God, made him a good counsellor.

I found that my life as a minute-man among the angels militant, and my subsequent service at Rivermouth, stood me in good stead, now that I needed to decide upon the course to pursue. I had been, when a child, powerfully drawn towards the ideal expressed in ancient text,—" My lord is wise, according to the wisdom of an angel." I had determined to know it all, some time; but with a certain orderliness, one thing at a time during unmeasured eons of after-ages.

" Order is heaven's first law," said Greylock. " The most mature and the least mature finite beings in the heavenly spheres must be so classified that the progress of advanced students and workers may not be retarded by too much contact with those who are but beginners in the schools of God. The heavenly sphere now occupied by Gabriel and his compeers, or one like it, will some time be yours, but that requires time.

" You are to seize upon the duty and privilege nearest to you, and then go up higher when you can sustain yourself in the higher career. You may go now to visit the sphere, where the most highly honored angels of God reside; and they will often come here for your instruction : but if you were to attempt to go there to live, and had no sense of your unfitness to do so to advantage, you would, after a little, be met with an inquiry whether you would not make more progress if you were to take a lower seat, in your appropriate sphere.

"It must seem to you reasonable that beings who have had to do with the affairs of God not only since the foundation of the world, but since the foundations of star systems preceding the material universe as we know it, must be wiser, according to the wisdom of the angels, than earth-born saints not yet a hundred years old."

CHAPTER SIXTH

RETURNING home, I sat with my brother, under
a great crag, upon one side of the garden, not
far from the falling water. We were a little
withdrawn from the soft light, that filled the
atmosphere with varying intensity like an electrical glow waning and increasing. The shrub-
bery was quite thick about us; and we kindled a
little fire, perhaps from old-time habit in frequent
living out-of-doors. My sister now joined us,
and I related to her what my mentor had said.

"Brother and I would like to know what those
angels do, who maintain their youth during ages
comparable with the self-existence of God."

"I learned much about it, in the sphere I last
visited; and it tallies well with what is taught
in the schools of this City."

Just then, mother came in. And a moment
after, father came with a stranger. Adding a
little fuel to the fire, I bade the stranger welcome
to sit with us.

His visit to this primary sphere was by an
invitation to give certain instruction, upon the

courses of study pursued in some of the spheres about us. Learning the topic we had begun to converse upon, he graciously entertained us with a brief summary which in part answered the question I had asked.

"I cannot tell you," he said, "when I was first conscious of being in heaven,—it is so long ago; long before Arcturus and the Pleiades were made. The planet upon which I was born, perished long before the birth of Orion, and if I were to say that there are some whose heavenly life has been thrice as long as mine, I should then say that there are others who even still more nearly approach the life of him who is from everlasting. As we say, 'in the beginning God created the heavens and the earth,' that is, the beginning of this system ; so we say of the angels, 'in the beginning' God created them. He revealed himself in the creation of finite mind, as in the creation of material forms. And those who are made in his image, who are the objects of his love, delight to call themselves the children of God; and in love and obedience they seek to fulfil his purposes.

"The topics of angelic study, and the angelic lines of action," continued our guest, "pertain to the self-revelation of God. For one thing, he has revealed himself in the constitution of finite minds, angelic or human.

"This mental constitution we study, as we find it in all worlds:—seeking to discern its powers; and its relation to the Mind of God; and its relation to the material instruments that it uses.

"We study too, to ascertain how superior minds can influence inferior, in a natural manner without disturbing the normal action of mental faculties.

"We learn also to measure with exactness the effect of external circumstances upon finite minds in every individual case; this being needful in deciding upon problems of moral conduct.

"And we study the truths most likely to be helpful to every child and man, who has it in him to become a child of immortality.

"We know when sinners repent: of all things that happen on earth, we not only know the external but we discern mental states.

"And we study how to introduce into the minds of men the ideas most helpful to them. This involves studies in philology, in literature, in the arts of expression, and methods in teaching.

"This department requires an unspeakable amount of investigation, and of record making, and systematic subdivision of labor,—including as it does the art of influencing finite minds in detail throughout the habitable universe.

"Those who seek to achieve mastery in God's service, as ministering spirits, as well as those who conduct the details of the work in this department, spend an incredible amount of time in the studies here indicated."

CHAPTER SEVENTH

WE were all privileged to attend the lectures given by him who had honored us by his presence. It appears that my father had met him, in his recent journeying, and that his eagerness to have us all make the most of our heavenly opportunity had prompted him to urge upon the stranger an hour's sitting at our camp-fire.

If not the first lectures in the course, yet those a little later I heard. And they gave further answer to my inquiry, as to the pursuits of the angels of God during the cycles of celestial time.

"One thing which occupies the angels," it was said by the speaker, "is the study of God's self-revelation in the physical creation. 'Marvellous are thy works, Lord God Almighty.'"

I cannot express how much of God he showed us in this natural revelation,—in sea and land, in storm and sunshine, in grass and flowers and fruit, in cedar and oak, in gold and silver and iron and precious stones, in mountains and caves of the earth, in rivers and waterfalls, in lakes and ocean currents, in fish and fowl and cattle, and in the animal natures of the children of immortality,—a revelation extending through all the stars that hang on high, innumerable as the sand grains on the shore of the sea.

I

And he who knew so well what the universe is like, chided us in gentle accents for speaking of the earth as the Land of Shadows. "It is the land of beauty," he said. "It is the land of sunshine. It is the land of joy,—and of sweet homes, of domestic loves, and holy friendships. Death is no evil: it is unbelief that is an evil; it is distrust of God that is an evil.; it is lack of spiritual vision that is an evil.

"O ye angels ministrant, do not tell the children of the weeping world that theirs is the Land of Shadows. It is a land but little removed from the heavenly state. O ye happy-hearted children of the heavenly King, can ye never persuade the children of earth, that they dwell upon the very confines of heaven, upon a globe that may be the very border-land of the ineffable glory? If they could only be persuaded to clean the earth, and to keep it clean,—to remove from it everything that worketh abomination and maketh a lie,—it would become a very suburb of the City of God.

"O child of the beautiful earth, thou child of the Land of the Dying, why spend your days in sighing for the sight of tall cataracts or gigantic mountains in far-away lands—for ere to-morrow eve you may visit the most famous world that hangs in the most distant heavens. · Are not all the provinces of God's celestial kingdom open before you ? Dost thou not know, O child of an immortal heritage, that the glittering constellations are as accessible to angelic wing, as the craggy tops of earthly mountains are to the eagles which fly above, while you toil wearily o'er the rough and steep ascent below ?

"O child of earth, dost thou leave thy native globe before thou knowest it altogether ? Know then, that thou shalt see it hereafter,—that in spiritual body thou shalt know it well; know it as the clouds and sunbeams know it, as the unseen powers of nature know it, — know it to manipulate it at will, under the guiding arm of the Almighty."

II

"The oldest of the angels," he said, "have a great interest in all the rising and falling spheres of what we call the temporary, the ma-

terial creation, to distinguish it from what, for
convenience, we call the spiritual, the eternal.
These heavenly spheres change not; since God
wills it so.   Other star systems rise and fall;
since God wills it so.   There is no force in natural law, to make this or that; what we call
natural law is but the observed method in which
the will of God acts.   And the transient cosmic
systems are so made from design that their evolution and their degradation will be perfected
in a few scores of millions of years; while the
eternal habitation of God and of spiritual beings
knows no increase or decay, since God wills
it so.

"What these laws are, that pertain to systems
celestial and terrestrial, and what constitutes the
difference between them, is one of the studies
of those who are the instruments of God; there
being laws supernatural, through which certain
material effects can be produced that do not
come within the province of laws natural.   There
are processes,—healing and life-giving, multiply-
ing, strengthening, preserving,—which are well
known as ordinary methods of God's working in
the realm supernatural, which are not in common
use in a system of things that is at best but
transient and that carries with it, its own decay.
These processes depend upon certain chemical
and physical properties; all of which are of use

in our supernatural realm, and a part of which
only are needed for the ordinary phenomena of
the realm of nature."

III

"It is the business of the angels," said the
lecturer, "to understand all secondary causes,
and to so understand them as to be able to use
them in really doing the works of God, in ma-
nipulating on some large scale the forces of the
universe. There is always much world-building
and fitting to do, to provide everlasting habi-
tations for new inhabitants who are coming
hither in every generation from far-off globes.
And there is constant demand for service in the
details of the rise and fall of the hundred million suns and their planets, that constitute the
material or natural universe.

"It is a principle in the heavens above, as in
the earth beneath, that Infinite wisdom and Infinite power delegates to finite beings everything
that they can learn to do. He who raised the
dead, asked men to roll away the stone. He who
could raise up children to Abraham from the
stones, chose rather to employ prophets and
preachers. In like manner, he trains angelic
beings during myriads of years, that they may

work the mighty works of God, so far as they can learn how to handle secondary causes.

"And it is a principle of Divine wisdom to bestow upon angels and men the power to gain knowledge; and then leave them to get it as best they can, by such means as he has furnished. Not in the heavens above or in the earth beneath does God impart knowledge, except through voluntary acquisition by the use of means that are at hand. There can be no idlers in the schools of God. And it requires ages upon ages of study, —of observation, reflection, experiments,—to become the Divine instruments in the realm of physics and chemistry.

"Nor can there be idlers in the schools of God if the standard of heaven is to be maintained, as to the mechanic arts, and the fine arts. The underlying principles must be understood by vast numbers of the celestial inhabitants. Our enthusiasm for excellence in music, in architecture, in painting, and in sculpture, must be kept at high pitch. Our experimental stations for work in all that relates to the mineral kingdom, and our gardens for the study of the vegetable kingdom, and for whatever relates to the animal kingdom, must be conducted by the highest intelligence obtainable in the several departments.

"How can beings here be fitted to act as the

instruments of the Creator, who are ignorant of the first principles of creation?

"And how can beings here be fitted for service as ministering angels, if they are ignorant of what it behooves them to know if they are to be of service? Must they not know at least certain conditions of health and disease? And must they not know those physical laws, both natural and supernatural, by which they can effectively reach the minds of those they would benefit? With spiritual bodies attuned to subtle laws, natural and supernatural, by which they can see through all things, by which they can penetrate all things, by which they can move as swiftly as thought, may they not indeed become the very instruments of God in realms material and spiritual, if their own minds are equal to solving the problems that confront them?"

IV

"This department of study, the self-revelation of God in the physical creation," it was further said, "requires the service of trained students to conduct it, and to arrange for instructing others. And it involves both observation and service in all parts of the universe. It is carried forward by numbers without number

of enthusiastic investigators and helpers; some
of whom have perhaps little special aptitude for
work like metaphysics or history, while others
are well equipped by all-round studies in every
department of heavenly lore."

V

Preceding and following the lectures upon this
department of study, there were concerts for
rendering music fitted to the theme; the ora-
torio of the Creation, and antiphonal singing in
the Psalms that celebrate the glory of God in his
handiworks.   Not less than three leagues square
was the standing-room area, occupied by the
chorus; who were arranged, however, in a semi-
circle and rising tiers about the director.

And the most excellent glory of the First
Cause of all things that were, and are, and are
to come, was made manifest to the eyes of all
beholders.

9

CHAPTER EIGHTH

I

God in history—the history of angels and men—this is another mode of God's self-revelation, which is a theme for angelic study. The lecturer indicated it to be the purpose of this department :—

To trace the story of God's providence in the moral evolution of man,—particularly the work of redemption :

To discover the principles underlying the moral government of God ;

And the principles of justice and right in what relates to national and social well-being :

To maintain a system of historic and biographic writing, by recording angels, who trace with sufficient fulness the details of celestial and human activity,—so that books may be opened at any moment, to find the standing of every individual before God.

II

These departments for studying God's self-revelation in mind, in nature, and in history, are conducted in connection with like systematic study of God's revelation of himself in writings which express the mind of the Spirit; writings, whether celestial, terrestrial, or pertaining to other worlds.

III

These courses of study, and of administrative service, which may well occupy one's time for untold myriads of years, are open to all who are fitted to enter upon them advantageously, either for long or short terms at will. Their definite design is to prepare those who are wise and prudent and competent, to act as the Divine instruments, in such service as any one may be qualified for.

IV

Both before and after these lectures upon the history of God's providential work upon the earth, and upon the written revelation of God, there were illustrative pageants and triumphant

processions throughout the streets of the City ;
rendering praise and thanksgiving and homage to
the Infinite Majesty, and lauding him who is the
King of Kings, the Moral Governor of the universe.   The prominent figures, in these displays
of worship, were the very personages who have
been the honored instruments of God in conducting the affairs of his kingdom.   And by the side
of every man so honored, there appeared that
guardian angel who had stood by him in his
earthly contests.

The music upon the closing day of special service of thanksgiving and triumph, was held in
what is known as the great amphitheatre of this
City of God : a vast area of many miles, gently
rising from the centre on every side, and surrounded by mountain slopes and peaks.   And in
reproducing the works of earthly and heavenly
masters to illustrate the history of God's majestic movements in the earth, the chorus occupied the whole of this area below and above.
And when the *Messiah* was rendered, the sky
above was filled with listening and singing angels,
who formed a canopy,—rising like a radiant dome
to a great height over the whole amphitheatre.
And the Lord Jesus appeared among them, and
the glory of God was manifest.

Book IV

THE LIGHT OF OUR FATHER'S LOVE

CHAPTER FIRST

I

NEXT morning, as I watched the eastern skies for swiftly changing clouds of purple and gold, the pinnacles of rock about me suddenly shone with unwonted brilliancy, as a resplendent being from another world alighted near me, whose countenance was like the lightning, and his raiment white as snow.

"The heavens are hung in purple and gold," he said, "to mark the dawn of the chief festal day of our celestial year, — the Marriage Supper of the Lamb. I hail thee, therefore, O son of earth, since to-day we celebrate the love of God to his earthly Church."

And for the hour he talked with me, to tell the story of Love Divine.

"It is eternal life," he said, "to know God. And during ages infinite, or far past all earthly telling or comprehension, during all revolving cycles of heavenly time, the angels of God have sought to know him. Nothing satisfies them save God alone. In all material glories of the

universe around us, and in the unfolding of
spiritual powers, we evermore long for God, to
repose in his love. Our search for infinite knowledge is but restlessness, unless as children we
find the Infinite Father and Friend. He is the
solace of all our days. The glory of our heavenly life is not without increasing splendor, since
it culminates in God. In seeking to know him,
we find all treasures of wisdom and knowledge.
This is the grand and all-absorbing occupation ;
offering bliss unspeakable, for ages endless.

"Yet, O child of earth, it is in thee, we find
new depths of Love Divine. We saw the rebel
angels fall, and there was no remedy. But while
the tribes of men were yet sinners, Christ died
for the ungodly."

II

No sooner did the angel leave me than I saw
my father approaching. And having told him
what was said to me, he replied,—

"I understand now what was once not clear to
me. Mutual love is the rule in heaven. There
is no separating selfishness. And the only way
in which God could restore our fallen race was
to introduce love as a common factor between
the sons of earth. No heaven on earth were otherwise possible. Looked at in a large way, it

comes to this : God is love; heaven is a place
where all the inhabitants love each other,—and
there they love God, and are beloved of him.
The expression of God's love to sinners in Jesus
Christ was needed, in order to introduce into
the world the idea of an unselfish love as the
solvent of all the ills of men.   It was, even to
the angels, a new discovery of the height and
depth and breadth of the love of God.

" And now," he added, after a moment's pause,
"we who were far off, are brought nigh by the
blood of Christ.   And all earthly distractions
have, for us, gone by forever.   And now the un-
interrupted companionship of God is as open to
us, as if we had been born without sin.

"It was when I was a mere boy, that I made
up my mind, one night, as I paced up and down
the river-bank, under the light of the winter
stars, that I would forego my intimacy with wild
and wicked youth around me, and that henceforth I would seek the Great Companion ; and
when I found him, I was content.   And now I
live and move and have my being in him.

"Nor is there for us anything, but to do as
the angels do,—to go through the heavenly life
looking upward.   It is God, God in Christ, in
whom we have joy unspeakable and full of glory.
Our spiritual powers are developed by reaching
towards nothing less than God.   That seraph

mounts highest, who fixes his eye solely on God.

"The greatest attraction of heaven is not found in its social life, or its social studies, or even its social and public worship when a few or all the throngs of angels meet for praise, or even in walking with Christ in company with a small band of disciples. We shall be little content to lead a life always in public, even if it be called heaven. Having been trained under a Bible full of personal pronouns, and personal promises, can we be satisfied with anything less than our God, and the personal love of Christ to us?

"The very words of God have inspired us to seek constantly the presence of the Only One, and can we rest in any other company? If on the earth, we were to sigh after God, then shall we in heaven be quiet? Can the God we so often met in our closets on earth, forsake us now that we have entered into his glory? Of what avail is the omnipresence of God, if every one who loves him cannot at times have choice hours alone with him?"

"These pinnacles of rock decided me," I replied. "Among many mansions, I am well satisfied to build here, a little apart from neighbors. Then, too, I have found out deep solitudes in the country about. I used to have such a sense of moral unfitness for the companionship of Infinite

Love and Purity, that I could not, so well as now, have that perfect love that casteth out fear; but here where I can daily see God, as if face to face, I long to be much alone with him, to bring all my thoughts into captivity to him, and to exult in his absolute dominion and universal sway. It is my prayer in every hour: 'Show us the Father, and it sufficeth us.'"

CHAPTER SECOND

I

IN the festivities of hours next following, my father was separated from us, being entitled to certain rank and honors that did not fall to us, on account of the stars in his crown of rejoicing. My brother accompanied my mother; and I went another way with my sister. She and I had been great friends in our early teens, and we were always together.

"My brother," she said, "this festal day always seems to me like my own wedding-day. And I have always wished that I could tell you what our Lord Jesus Christ has been to me personally, since I came to this country;—came alone as you remember, the first one from our house. I was old enough to have great ideals and lofty aspirations, and I was still so young as to know little of the difficulties that might stand between me and my ambitions. Now I had no sooner come here, than our Lord met me, much as if he had been my Elder Brother; and he has always been my dearest Friend, as

much so as if there were none other to share his
love.   His Divine attribute of omnipresence is
manifested here, as it could not be upon the
earth without producing confusion.   And here
we behold him in some real and appropriating
sense, as much as if he were not elsewhere present: so that he is to every redeemed soul the
Heavenly Bridegroom, and him we love with a
passion of devotion.

"So our God tempers to us the heavenly glories,—not blinding our eyes at once with that
awful vision before which angels veil themselves;
but he dawns upon us in the person of Jesus
who is to us the Sun of Righteousness.   The
day is breaking, the dawn is shining, the sky
is glowing,—and soon the ineffable Majesty of
the Ancient of Days will be seen by us with un-
dimmed eyes, as the principalities of other worlds
behold him.

"He who made first the blade, then the ear,
then the full corn in the ear; he who tempered
his words to his disciples, 'I have many things
to say unto you, but ye cannot bear them now;'
he who unfolded a little at a time the scheme of
his earthly kingdom to the glorious company of
the apostles;—will reveal to us the glories of his
Father's house, according to our capacity to receive it.

"It is written that he who is in the midst of

the throne shall lead us unto living fountains of
waters; for with him is the fountain of life.
And we shall follow the Lamb whithersoever he
goeth."

II

And as we so conversed, the path we walked
was lightened with the glory of an angel who
was approaching us. He it was, who had hos-
pitably entertained my sister and my mother on
their late journeying upon another sphere celestial.

"I remember," he said, after an exchange of
greetings, "that glory of the Son of God, which
he had with the Father before the world was.
And now I am come to behold the glory which
he bestows upon his people in making them the
house-mates of God, as if united to the Great
Companion of the soul, who has said,—'I have
loved thee with an everlasting love, and I will
betroth thee to me forever, in righteousness, in
judgment, in loving-kindness, in mercies—I
will betroth thee unto me in faithfulness.'

"Welcome, and welcome again, O children of
the Land of Shadows, to the Light of our Father's Love. Ye are they who heard the voice
of Jesus,—'I call you not servants but friends;
and whosoever doeth the will of my Father which

is in heaven the same is my brother and sister and mother.'

"All hail, ye who are next of kin to the Son of God. Joy be to you, concerning whom God has said, 'I thy Maker am thy husband.' Come hither, O bride, behold the Marriage Supper is ready. Come, ye who are members of his body, come and eat of the hidden manna, come drink of the fruit of the vine in our Father's Kingdom.

"To-day, the angel hosts are glad and rejoice, and give honor to our Lord; for the Marriage of the Lamb is come, and his wife hath made herself ready,—and blessed are they which are called unto the Marriage Supper of the Lamb. These are the true sayings of God."

And in like manner, there came forth the angels of God from other spheres to meet those earth-born angels for whom Christ died; they met each little company, in coming forth from their several mansions, and gave greeting on behalf of the Son of God,—and led them forward to that place where they were to meet the Heavenly Bridegroom.

CHAPTER THIRD

I

IT is written that "the righteous shall shine forth as the sun in the kingdom of their Father." Yet I was little prepared to see the ranks of the glorified in such radiant garments, with faces like the sun. Then I saw that the glory of the Lord had risen upon them; and that the Lord was their everlasting light. The light of love in every heart was glowing.

Then I saw one, having the form of the Son of Man, appearing far away in the distant skies, shining in clouds of glory with a brilliance surpassing the sun. And all eyes were turned upward to behold his approach. And every form reflected the supernal light.

And I heard a voice divine, saying, "I am the Light of the world; he that followeth me shall have the light of life."

Then all the angels of God who were natives of heaven, answered in a loud voice,—"And ye are the light of the world." And then there appeared a great wonder in heaven,—a woman clothed with the sun, and the moon under her feet, and upon her head a crown of stars.

And there appeared above them a roof of clouds as white as snow, and around them were pillars of gleaming gold, as if the temple of the Highest enclosed them.

Then as the vision faded, the sky was filled with the brightness of the Father's glory, as if I could see God face to face.

II

And instantaneously, the skies in all heights above and upon the north afar, and on the south and the east and the west, were crowded with the ranks of the choirs of God. And I, so dumb upon the earth, found myself among them.

Upon the sides of the north, far above the City of God, even to the fountains of the River of Peace, extended the singing hosts of God's earthly Church, arrayed in robes of righteousness bestowed upon her by the Heavenly Bridegroom; and upon the sides of the east and of the west, were the Archangels and the Cherubim and Seraphim, and the great leaders of song in all the musical spheres of heaven, with instruments without number; and upon the sides of the south, I saw the Four-and-twenty Elders,

10

and the Four Living Ones who surround the throne of the Infinite Majesty, and I saw the Authorities, and Dominions, and Principalities, and Powers, and the thrones of those who are the instruments of God in the administration of his creative work and the moral government of the universe.

And all those mighty angelic personalities of hoary ages covered their faces, at the vision of a white cloud and the Ancient of Days, with his many crowns, and head as white as snow, and eyes like a flame, and countenance like the sun, and his raiment white as the light,—a vision flashing out for a moment.

Then I saw a mighty angel come down from the highest heaven, clothed with a radiant cloud, and a rainbow was upon his head, and his face was as it were the sun, and his feet as pillars of fire; and he bore a crown of thorns.

III

Then there rose from the sides of the north a new song, from the redeemed of every nation and kindred and tongue and people, ten thousand times ten thousand and thousands of thousands:

" Worthy is the Lamb that was slain, to receive

power, and riches, and wisdom, and strength, and honor, and glory, and blessing."

And then from the sides of the south, and the east, and the west, arose the chorus—

"Blessing, and honor, and glory, and power, be unto him that sitteth upon the throne, and unto the Lamb for ever and ever."

And then in tidal flow of song, that great multitude whom no man can number on the sides of the north, clothed in white robes and palms in their hands, cried with a loud voice, saying,—

"Salvation to our God, which sitteth upon the throne, and unto the Lamb."

And now all the heavenly hosts, with golden harps in their hands, sang the song of Moses and the Lamb, saying,—

"Great and marvellous are thy works, Lord God Almighty; just and true are thy ways, thou King of saints. Who shall not fear thee, O Lord, and glorify thy name? For thou art holy; for all nations shall come and worship thee; for thy judgments are made manifest."

Then there rose like a great wailing cry from the north,—"Unclean, unclean." Then quickly rose the jubilant cry,—"But holy, holy, is the Lord God Almighty; and worthy is the Lamb that was slain, to receive power, and riches, and wisdom, and strength, and honor, and glory, and blessing."

Then I heard the singing angels of God, upon the south,— "What are these which are arrayed in white robes, and whence came they?"

And they upon the east and upon the west made answer,— "These are they which came out of great tribulation, and have washed their robes, and made them white in the blood of the Lamb."

Then sang all the heavenly host,— "Therefore are they before the throne of God, and serve him day and night in his temple: and he that sitteth on the throne shall dwell among them."

And then from the north rang out the glad song,— "Glory and dominion unto him that loved us, and washed us from our sins in his own blood; and hath made us kings and priests unto God."

IV

Now all the tuneful ranks were broken; and the hosts of God, descending from their skies of song, overflowed the City of God, the new Jerusalem,—settling for the moment upon all the garden lands and mountain peaks and the many mansions of our Father's house, and extending far and wide upon the great plain lands and meadows of Peace. And everywhere their songs arose: and I heard as it were the voice of a great

multitude, and as the voice of many waters, and
as the voice of mighty thunderings, saying,—

"Alleluia: for the Lord God omnipotent reign-
eth. Let us be glad and rejoice, and give honor
to him: for the marriage of the Lamb is come,
and his wife hath made herself ready. Blessed
are they which are called unto the Marriage
Supper of the Lamb."

V

Nor was there need, in all this day, for the
shining of the sun in our Father's house, for the
Lord God was the Light thereof.

And when all our visitants arose and swiftly
made their way to other spheres of light, then
the people of God went forth in search for solitudes, where they might kindle their twilight
camp-fires; that they might gather around them,
and sing their old songs, and tell their stories of
battle and conquest, and render in every place
their thanksgiving to God Most High for his re-
deeming love.

CHAPTER FOURTH

EVERYWHERE the ancient cathedral bells were ringing, and everywhere the camp-fires were blazing, and everywhere were heard the sounds of gladness. Yet I could not join the joyous peoples, till I had first sought out the Lord alone :—

"O Friend of sinners, is it said, that the bride hath made herself ready? I have never made myself ready; but thou hast made me ready, by casting over me the robe of thy righteousness."

"Be still, my child. The bride hath made herself ready by accepting the gift of God to the penitent."

"Oh, my Father," I cried, "I am not worthy to be called the bride of the Heavenly Bridegroom. Make me as one of thy servants."

"Rise up, O child; the penitent prodigals of earth are not called hither to be menials at the King's court, but companions in the King's house."

"Who would have thought," I said, when I joined my comrades, "that we, who knew so little of the love of God, and whose prayers were often blind, and who knew not how to pray, and who made so many sad mistakes in the way to heaven, should now be loved and comforted, as God comforteth his people ?"

I never knew the earthly name of him who answered me :—

"It was, indeed, no vain thing that we struggled on there below,—trying to make Christ our most intimate Friend. We were even then, as we were told, members of his flesh. And by solitary communion with him, we grew into his acquaintance and his love. And sometimes we were lonely, longing for the presence of Jesus, and crying, —'There is none upon the earth that I desire besides thee : And now I cry,—'whom have I in heaven but thee ?'

> "'A heaven without my Saviour
>   Would be no heaven to me ;
> Dark were the walls of jasper,
>   Rayless the crystal sea.'"

II

Although I had been in heaven for some years, yet this was the first festal day of the so-called Marriage Supper that I had attended,—having been sent elsewhere upon varied service.

And I could but shrink a little from being called by the endearing name chosen by God's love, to express the nearness to him, of his earthly disciples,—the union of holy spirits with a holy God. Yet I had begun long ago, in self-renunciation oft repeated, to form the habit of disinterested self-sacrifice. It was however hard for me to see, that this too was the gift of God. And he to whom a disciple was peculiarly "beloved," has apparently delighted in making characters worthy of being loved,—making them so by his transforming and perfecting grace.

The grandeur and glory of our Saviour's character, its beauty and its purity, I had long known; but his tenderness, his loving sympathy, his warm affection, I knew not until I came here. And I shall never be satisfied till I am conformed to his likeness.

III

He who had been my guardian angel, before I came hither, was one of those I found at our twilight camp-fire.

"God is training," he said, "his earthly Church to become a part of that celestial society which he will enjoy forever; the relation being much like that of children to a parent,—children forever growing, and age after age becoming more like God. Our Redeemer has therefore chosen to represent the children of grace as his companions in glory. And forevermore it will be his delight to see their characters unfolding, and to see them more and more conformed to his image, and on their part taking more and more comfort in his society as their best Friend."

IV

With joy unspeakable and full of glory, we greatly rejoiced in the Lord, who clothed us with the garments of salvation. And the glad hours swiftly passed in thanksgiving and the voice of melody.

"What I have desired, now I see," said one; "what I have hoped for, now I hold; what I have longed for, now I possess."

And with the rising sun, every man greeted
his neighbor, with fitting salutation,—" Blessed
be Jesus Christ ;" and for the answer, " Forever,
and forever.   Amen."

V

Upon this crowning festal day, our Lord was
alone with the people of his redemption; all
upon this sphere gathering now to meet him.

Amid clouds of incense appeared the Lord
Jesus, extending his arms in blessing as he de-
scended to meet his expectant disciples, who had
seen him in like manner ascend, after his holy
passion.   And upon this day, the raiment of our
Lord was like that worn by the Master in his
earthly mission.

Nor was there, upon this day, any singling out
of patriarchs and prophets and kings, who had
desired to see his day, nor the fathers and founders of the Church, nor martyrs and saints, nor
heroes, nor men of high rank in the Church militant.   No one upon this day was called rabbi;
but all were brethren, standing in common relation to their one Master.

" This is my body broken for you ;" " This is
my blood in the new testament, shed for many,
for the remission of sins :" this was the simple
service of the Marriage Supper of the Lamb.

And as the bride is henceforth known by a new name, so our Lord gave to each of us, who had not before received it, a white stone, and in the stone a new name written,—a name untarnished by sin, a name to be made honorable in a new career ; a white stone, as a personal pledge in earthly custom, entitling every one who receives it, to call on him who gives it, for all needful aid in every hour.

With such pledge to his loved ones, and with a hymn of thanksgiving, the supper was ended.

VI

Yet the myriads who had gathered, throughout the livelong day and twilight hours, were continually praising and blessing God; singing for joy of heart, in the heights of Zion. Nor eye hath seen, nor ear heard, nor hath entered into the heart of man to conceive the glory of being forever with the Lord ; where Love is enthroned, in our home in glory,—to live with him and to reign with him.

Book V

THE MINISTERING ANGELS

CHAPTER FIRST

I WENT away to the mountains at the fountain-head of the River of Peace, to spend the twilight hours. Building a little fire next a great crag, I was there many hours alone with Him whom my soul loveth. And it was from this great height that I saw the sun rise.

This mass of mountains is arranged in the form of a horseshoe, with streams everywhere descending between the peaks, to form the great river. The area within the shoe is like an upland mountain plateau of great extent. Except near the bases of the mountains, it is comparatively level. And many of the streams that form the main river are relatively of good size, with broad margins of meadow as they approach the River of Peace. The foot-hills abound in beautiful groves, and the banks of the streams below are well shaded.

At sunrise, I saw that there was to be at once a great assembly in this vast amphitheatre; and soon perceived that it was a Conference of the Ministering Angels,—many of them from other spheres of light.   The gathering was, however, in relatively small sections,—those delegated to a specific service; each indeed comprising many thousands, and even tens of thousands in some departments.   Everywhere I saw the council-fires kindling, and comrades gathering about them.

I visited the vast pine lands, just above where the main river is formed by the junction of two large streams.   Extending throughout these cathedral woods, I found a large encampment of those who are novices in earthly ministration; and with them, for their instruction, were angelic teachers from other spheres.

Joining myself to a camp-fire circle at the point where the streams meet, I discovered a company who were learning the merest rudiments of their contemplated work.   In garments whiter than snow, and with wings of gold, their teacher stood; his face as mobile as a living flame,—recalling to my mind the word of God, that he hath made his ministers a flaming fire.

I

"My children," said the angel, "ye are they whom God hath called from earth,—his service requiring you so swift for messages Divine.   He

saw your eager and almost impatient anxiety to
do his will in all things.   And some of you, I
fear, burned out your lives too soon.   Our God
hath need of you; there is always service for
those who rest not.

"Have ye not heard of the Four Living Ones,
who rest not day nor night, saying, 'Holy, holy,
holy, Lord God Almighty, which was, and is,
and is to come'?   In entering heaven, you have
come to a busy place.   We rest not day nor
night, and yet we are not weary.   Toil is but a
joy to the sons and daughters of the Almighty.
Perfect repose is found in the ceaseless activity
of all our powers; every faculty in frictionless
action, intense and harmonious as the wheeling
stars in their courses.   Employment is the enjoyment of heaven.   An idle air would weary the
wing of the angels.

"What hurrying to and fro of messengers
there is, about the court of the Ruler of the universe, you may see and know from the thousand
thousands who minister unto him, and ten thousand times ten thousands who stand before him;
the shining ones in sandals of golden light, whose
loins are girt, who stand and wait,—the ministers
of God who do his pleasure.

"These are they who are at one with God in
purpose, who keep his commandments with such
delight, that our Lord Jesus could make no

11

prayer for the earth more fitting than that God's
will might be done on earth as it is in heaven.
It is a service so sweetly toned, and so varied, as
to be like a great instrument, responding perfectly to the master's touch, in rendering harmonious worship,—the praise of God by all the
activities of which finite beings are capable; a
worship so perfect in obedience, that if, as one
of your own number has said, two angels were
commanded, the one to govern an empire, and
the other to sweep a street in it, they would not
desire a change of employments."

II

At this moment I discovered my Helen to
be of this company; and in my ecstasy of
joy, I did not further note the words of the
angel.

"Why, father," she said, after our first greetings. "I did not know that heaven was so near
to the earth. It is but one step out of the body
into the realms of light. It seemed as if I saw a
ladder with the angels of God ascending and descending, and grandmother stood at the bottom
of it. Then uncle A. caught me in his arms, and
the vision faded, and I am here. It was like re-
moving a veil, and heaven was the other side of

it. But I have not found out yet how to see beyond the veil, to look back again."

"The principle of life," I said in reply, "is closely related to particles of the cosmic ether. I do not know how. But it is so related to it, that the spirit, when once free from the body, can instantly penetrate everything that is interpenetrated by the particles of ether. And there is a third dimension, by which it is possible to see through all substances, so that the great cloud of witnesses can discern all earthly activity as God sees it. We can tell even what men are thinking about,—their spiritual attitude before God. You have come unto an innumerable company of angels, who act as ministering ones,— operating like the secret forces of nature, in perfect accord with physical laws, and never disturbing or contravening the ordinary forces. So men are influenced in a natural manner, without knowing that they are wrought upon by Divine ministration."

III

At this point, we saw that the novices were crowding around their teacher, eagerly questioning him.

"This Training School for Ministering Spirits," he said in reply, "is the best department opened

in this primary sphere. The principle is this:
you know how hard the struggle is in the Land
of Shadow, and God on his part intends to extend
his help. In his general scheme, therefore, for
governing the universe, he has ordained that
those who seek to do God's will in heaven, shall
help those who seek to do God's will on earth.
There can be nothing more reasonable than this.

"By a subtle law, analogous to that of magnetic
attraction, the heavenly help is rendered to those
who are in an attitude to receive it. Those who
are willing to do God's will on earth are, in virtue
of their willingness, in such attitude, that those
willing to do God's will in heaven can help them.

"This scheme, then, of angelic ministration,
has a regular place, as one of the subdivisions of
ordinary service in the Divine administration of
the moral universe. A large and well-organized
force is always at hand, under the management
of one of the Principalities.

"This accords with the Divine principle of
working through instruments, by general laws
and secondary causes, and it serves two important ends: the one, that of succoring those who
need their help; the other, that of developing
the powers of those who so minister. ·

"Upon the earth God helped you, by teaching you to help yourselves. That is what he
does now. To have a myriad angels settle down,

and abide in one compact city, wearing white robes and singing psalms,—is not heaven. It is heaven to develop the powers of God's people, making them wise according to the wisdom of the angels; and there is no better way than to set them to work, to aid the moral development of the planet from which they came,—definite work for definite persons.

"To this end, there is a constant going to and fro, of the messengers of God, throughout this sphere, to ascertain the exact facts. Information is gathered, as to the desires of God's people here, in respect to the earth from which they came; then systematic attention is given to the work of meeting those desires. While there is a general plan to help the earth, yet the proffered help must be definite; and those who come hither, give information, and they present requests, and they volunteer service.

"Then there are great gatherings, or Conferences, such as you see here now,—for hearing reports, and for consultation."

IV

And now the whole company, about this camp-fire, fell to singing their old hymns, and the new songs they had already learned in heaven.

Meantime, my daughter and I had an interview with the angel, who had been our teacher.

"Can we, then," Helen asked, "directly modify the lives of our dear ones, without their hearing our mystic wings?"

"You can, in a measure, be the instruments of our Father's hand in leading them from the Land of Shadow to the Light of our Father's House."

"What is the best form of service?" I asked.

"That which you are now best fitted for," he answered. "Then when you are fitted for something else, try that. There is a variety of administration. We have no monotonous round of duty, which would tend only to form a tedious sameness of character that would prove very wearying as the ages go by; but each one retains his individuality, and seeks to develop his peculiar powers,—doing what we can do best. The angels all differ,—as one star from another; there are not two alike in heaven. So the tree of life has leaves of the same general character, but they differ in minute outline; and the tree has twelve manner of fruits.

"I was myself once a Jewish rabbi, and I say now what I used to say: that every angel has a tablet on his heart in which the name of God is combined with the name of the angel; and that this name indicates the character of his peculiar

ministry.   If it be not so, yet the symbol is right,
—since every one's mission is known to himself
and to God only.

"This angelic ministration is as varied in its
activity as the providence of God; and as di-
versified as the grace of God.

"If I may give you counsel, it will be this:
that you go about among all the encampments
that you find here.   They represent but a small
part of the ministering service that God delegates
to those spirits who seek to be his instruments.
These camps are, however, gathered according to
principles of classification suggested by the Old
and the New Testaments, as to what the Ministering Spirits do; so arranged here and now, that
they may fall in with what the earth-born angels
knew before they came here.

"If you go about among these camps, you can
tell what kind of work you can do best."

CHAPTER SECOND

I

THE first encampment we visited was under the
banner of the Angel of Repentance. The words
of our Lord were wrought upon its folds,—
"There is joy in heaven." It is the purpose
of this organization, to give joy to heaven and
earth by persuading men to subject their lives
to the law of love, as followers of Jesus Christ.

The great company under this banner, extended far up and down both banks of the main
river, and the lower parts of its affluents ; spread-
ing out over the meadows, and plains of the second bank. Everywhere the shade was abun-
dant ; and it seemed as if all the birds of Paradise
were singing in their glad company.

Here we met my father, who had much to say
about this particular host of ministering ones.
With him we visited that island in the River of
Peace, where the silver bells are always ringing
to proclaim the glad news of earthly penitence.
It was far down the river, where the palm-trees

flourish; and we stood upon a hill-top, overlooking broad reaches of relatively still water.

The telegraphic system of the universe has a station here, and the bell chimes are never silent. We saw David Livingstone coming in, to learn the news from Africa.

"How many there are," my father said, "with whom we used to sympathize in their hours of temptation, whom we sought to help in their self-contending; and we will help them now."

II

In visiting the different camp-fires in this department, we found the work highly organized. Upon one bank of the main river, one company of workers; and those engaged in different work, upon the other bank. Then the coming in of a stream marked a subdivision in the great encampment. And in following up the various affluents a little distance, we came to other hosts conferring upon other parts of the same great work. At every camp-fire we found the banner of the Angel of Repentance, which had, besides its motto, the insignia of John the Baptist, who had presided at this Conference last session.

My daughter could be hardly persuaded to go from one camp-fire to another, since each one had so much to interest her. "Here," she said, "I will build a tabernacle, and abide. It is good to be here."

This was at the camp for the Fulfilment of the Prophecy; where the prophet Isaiah, the prophet Daniel, and the apostle John, were the leading spirits in the consultations of the hour.

And here we found a great host singing :—

"The Gentiles shall come to thy light, and kings to the brightness of thy rising. To Zion I will extend peace like a river, and the glory of the Gentiles like a flowing stream. And the kingdom and dominion, and the greatness of the kingdom under the whole heaven, shall be given to the people of the saints of the Most High, whose kingdom is an everlasting kingdom, and all dominions shall serve and obey him."

The next camp-fire we visited was upon another stream. It was a gathering of the Angels of the Churches. Some had been pastors, perhaps recently, or even centuries ago. And among them there were frequent changes, the same angel not long remaining with the same Church.

We found one camp-fire, that was surrounded by the representatives of myriads of the Angels of Christian Consistency, who seek to be the instruments of the Holy One for the sanctification of the Church. The apostle James was their presiding officer; and their banner bore the legend,

—"These are they which follow the Lamb whithersoever he goeth."

The next camp was that of the Working Church. Its motto was this: "So built we the wall; for the people had a mind to work." And the stalwart Nehemiah was their leader. And every angel in this company wore, as a symbol upon his breast, some building tool, crossed by some weapon of war.

We lingered long in the camp of the Proclamation; where we saw the banner of the Angel and the Trumpet. The leader was that mighty angel, whom the Revelator saw, flying in the midst of heaven, having the everlasting Gospel to preach unto them that dwell on the earth, to every nation and kindred and tongue and people, saying with a loud voice: "Fear God, and give glory to him,—for the hour of his judgment is come; and worship him that made heaven, and earth, and the sea, and the fountains of waters."

Here, we found many of the great evangelists, the Wesleys, the Whitefields, of the earthly Church. And here my father remained, to converse with Nettleton and Jonathan Edwards in regard to revival work.

Pressing forward, with Helen, I soon saw the colors of the Heavenly Dove. And we heard the chorus,—"The Spirit and the Bride say 'Come.'"

And here we saw the Angel of the New Birth; and an exceeding great following of those who desire to be the instruments of God in urging upon the consciences of men such phases of truth as may lead them to spiritual decision, and who seek to surround men with circumstances that may favor their spiritual renewal. And here, too, we found many who, having failed of persuading some of their own friends to live nobler lives and to dedicate themselves to God only, were now eager to win them at last with angelic art and tones of celestial love. And here, too, were some who had sought for self-denying toil in mission fields, and whose plans had been broken, who now stand clothed with heavenly might upon the distant coast or in the mountain district, and who toil there unseen and unrequited by mortals,—those elect angels who "contented with their fame in heaven seek not the praise of men."

III

Two camps were to me of peculiar interest. One was that of the Guides; where he, whom we once called St. Philip, was the leader. Here were the angels whose business it is, to direct persons into the ways of usefulness; to give monitions quite directly to speak to such and such a person, in aid of his spiritual life.

The other was the camp of the Angel of Prayer. As we entered, reports were being made. And here we saw the angel with whom Abraham pleaded for Sodom, and him with whom Israel wrestled in the night; him who visited Cornelius, and him, who, of most honored name, flew swiftly to answer the prayer of Daniel the prophet. None, indeed, were here but the oldest of the angels, those most experienced in the affairs of earth, those having the most wisdom and the most power to act as the instruments of the Spirit in helping the infirmities of devout men, and imparting to them suggestions that are indeed Divine.

And here I beheld the symbol set forth by him to whom men ought always to pray, lifting up holy hands without sin and without doubting :—

When the sun had gone down behind the mountains, I saw the Angel of Prayer approach the altar with a golden censer; and there was given unto him much incense, that he should offer it with the prayers of all saints upon the golden altar; and the smoke of the incense, with the prayers of the saints, ascended up before God out of the angel's hand.

In this holy place of prayer we lingered all the twilight hours: listening to the tales of

those who traverse the most benighted portions
of the Land of Shadows—where the moral darkness may be felt,—in order day by day to search
out all true worshippers, and carry their prayers
to the throne of God.

CHAPTER THIRD

WHEN the sun was up, we went to the oaks that thrive on the lower slopes of the mountains, which look out upon the meadows and streams below. These uplands of oak extend on every side of the vast amphitheatre; and they were everywhere occupied by the Angels of the Christian Warfare.

As we went from point to point, throughout the circuit, we noticed very few of the earth-born angels; they were rather of the elder sons of God, who sang with the morning-stars of the earlier creations.

I

There were three general subdivisions. The first we visited, were called the Pioneers. It is their calling to guide pilgrims from the Land of Shadows to the Light of our Father's House.

He who has said,—"This is the way, walk ye in it," has also said that he will give his angels charge, to keep thee in all thy ways; and they shall bear thee up in their hands, lest thou dash thy foot against a stone.

These are the angels who are the servants, the attendants, of the people of God, in the house of their pilgrimage. By them those who journey are directed in their way; as, to this or to that person; or to this or that destiny,—as an angel guided Joseph from his patriarchal home into Egypt, that he might there fulfil the behests of God.

It was here, that I met Dr. Philip Doddridge, whose hymns my daughter used to sing; and whose *Rise and Progress* I used to read.

"When I first came here," the doctor said, "I was at once ushered into a spacious apartment, the walls of which were adorned with pictures of what transpired in my own earthly life. And in each, I saw that I had been accompanied by angels at every step of my pathway, to guard me from danger, and to guide my feet into paths of peace. And then, as I stood looking over this panorama of my life, the Lord Jesus entered, and partook with me of the fruit of the vine newly pressed, and bade me welcome to his home on high.

"It is on this account," he added, after we had paused a moment to listen to the sweet singing that floated down from some point higher up the mountain-side, "on this account, I have attached myself to this company, that I may often walk up and down my old home in the sea-girt isle, to guide many in a way they know not, yet in a path that will certainly lead them home to God. I lead many in hard, toiling ways; I lead some through paths beset by temptation; and many through dark, very dark roads of sorrow; yet, I lead them all where duty calls, and I keep them from straying out of the rough and narrow way."

II

We next went to the encampments of the Armor-bearers.

Their duty it is, to afford protection to the heirs of salvation. Their fires were blazing all along upon the eastern side of the amphitheatre of Peace. These were, for the most part, the heaven-born angels; with great numbers of valiant spirits who well know earth's dangers, and who are in training for this service.

Here we saw those mighty beings who snatched Lot from Sodom, who walked into the furnace with the Hebrew youths, who locked the mouths of lions, who led Peter from prison, and who stood by Paul on the sinking ship.

Here, now, I met again John Bunyan, who had been but recently transferred to this service.

12

"So long," he said, "as we are in harbor, and they in storm,—we at rest, and they in the wilderness,—we are in duty bound to help them who are set about by perils in every moment of their lives. 'Tis said, that, of our Lord, 'the whole family in heaven and earth is named.' It is one and the same family; a part here, a part there. We, here, are bound to help them there, if they need our succor."

And then I espied Andrew Fuller, who has been long engaged in making suggestions to leading characters on earth, to ward off persecution, to concede the rights of conscience, to deliver from peril the lives of missionaries.

"Much depends upon the humor of individuals," I heard him say; "and I seek to influence them by invisible agency. A simple turn of thought in some leading mind in a province or nation, sometimes gives a favorable turn to the affairs of the people of God."

"It is perfectly safe," he added, when conversing with Bunyan, "for the child of God to go straightforward into the fire, or into the dens of beasts, or into prison-houses. Wherever his duty calls, let him advance; and he may hear his angel whispering peace,—'Though a thousand fall at thy side, and ten thousand at thy right hand, it shall not come nigh thee.'"

Then my daughter broke forth into singing.

It was an old song, that she learned when a
child :—

WATCH AND WARD

Soft the light of morning breaketh,
    Angel pinions haste away ;
Swift my soul from slumber waketh,
    New the guard that waits by day.

Soft the shade of night is falling ;
    Angel guards are hast'ning flight,
Loudly to their comrades calling,—
    They who watch me in the night.

Watch and ward, their turn are keeping
    Guardian angels, two and two ;
Waking cares, or careless sleeping,—
    God is watching fast and true.

III

Next we visited the Guards Militant, far over
among the oaks of the western side of the amphitheatre of Peace.   The greater part here, were of
the earth-born angels, under experienced leaders
from other spheres of light.

Here, we saw one of the chief princes, Michael
the archangel, who was the leader of this host
at this one gathering ; he who had so distin-
guished himself when there was war in heaven,
in fighting against the dragon, that old serpent,

called the Devil, and Satan, which deceiveth the
world ; that great prince, who stood for the people of Israel,—and who often participates in the
affairs of men at great epochs.

Here, too, we saw that mighty spirit who stood
with flaming sword to keep fallen man from
paradise.

Here, too, the captain of the guards of Elisha,
at the hill of Dothan, when the mountain was
full of horses, and chariots of fire, around about
the prophet of the Highest.

Here, too, we saw that archangel who commanded the sixty thousand angels, who were in
waiting when our Lord Jesus voluntarily laid
down his life for us, that he might take it again ;
that silent army, reposing in the skies, since their
Lord did not need them.

IV

" Oh, how I wish," cried Helen, "that mother
could see this great encampment.   How safe she
would feel!"

"She has the arms of Jesus," I replied. "She
loves him more than any other being in the universe.   And he is the nearest and the dearest of
friends.   And she tries to busy herself in service
for him, until he come."

"Now I see," said my daughter, "how true it is that God's people have a retinue of angels. Their wings have overshadowed us in the morning, the evening, and the midnight."

"Yes," I answered, " our God so shut us in, and kept us within the fold of Christ, by angels militant."

Then we looked up and saw that a great body of the Guards were moving swiftly up the mountain-side, in some evolution unknown to us. And they bore upon their banner the device :—

"The angel of the Lord encampeth round about them that fear him, and delivereth them."

Then I heard the sound of harping in the skies above me, and I heard a great company singing :—

"Some trust in chariots, and some in horses, but we will remember the name of the Lord our God, in his name will we set up our banners."

Then my daughter chanted the old English song :—

"How oft do they their silver bowers leave
 To come to succor us that succor want !
 How oft do they with golden pinions cleave
 The flitting skies, like flying pursuivant,
 Against foul fiends to aid us militant !
 They for us fight, they watch and duly ward,
 And their bright squadrons round about us plant ;
 And all for love and nothing for reward :
 O, why should heavenly God to me have such regard !"

CHAPTER FOURTH

WE next visited the encampment of the Authorities and Thrones, who are the rulers of nations.

Their fire was blazing far up the northern mountain-side, among the dark fir-trees; with immense crags beetling above them, and a far outlook opening below them,—as if they had built an eagle's eyrie for their place of rest.

They were few in number,—but a handful; of the oldest and most experienced of all the angels of God, who had seen long service in other departments of celestial activity before the foundation of the world.

It was in the twilight that we came hither; and we were warmly welcomed first to one great camp-fire, and then to another,—more heartily welcomed perhaps than would have been earthly kings who had little mind to obey God.

The hours were filled with music; the songs rehearsing the works the Almighty had committed to angelic hands in this department of service.

First, we heard a great multitude of the heavenly hosts, singing the glad news of redemption to a fallen world; the self-same voices that rang out upon the table-lands of Judea, when Jesus was born.   Then we heard the angels of the resurrection and the ascension of our Lord, with all manner of instruments glorifying the blessed Redeemer; the music representing the opening of the gates of death, and the uplifting of the everlasting doors for the King of glory to come in.

Then we heard the Angels of Revelation, celebrating that intellectual illumination, which was their gift from God to prophets and apostles and the leaders of the Church in all ages.   This service of song was accompanied by a swiftly changing series of visions: beginning with picturing the panorama of creation, as it appeared to Moses, the man of God; and certain scenes prophetic followed, and typical visions once displayed on Patmos; and then certain pictures illustrating the great epochs of new ideas in the story of the Church.   What was so expressed to the eye, was also set forth by appropriate music.   It was like seeing and hearing the Word of God in its making.   And when I saw an angel flying swiftly to him who figured one of the prophets—"Unto thee am I now sent, I am come forth to give skill and understanding," — and when the angelic choir burst forth into songs, descriptive of the

Spirit of Prophecy which sent forth the angels
to show unto the servants of God the things which
must shortly be done,—then I could see with
what power the Almighty had established the
throne of his eternal triumph in the earth.

Then I heard the songs of those who were
appointed of God to raise up or to pull down
earthly nations, to stir up war, or proclaim peace
among men,—those to whom the wrath of man is
made a vassal. Strange were the visions flashing against the dark mountain-side; angels mid
heaven with swords of fire, or some being appearing as of erst to the prophets of God,—to
determine the times of men. And the skies
were filled with orchestral music, and a single
voice I heard in song :—

"To him that overcometh will I give to sit with me in
my throne ; he that overcometh and keepeth my words to
the end, to him will I give power over the nations,—and I
will give to him the morning star."

"To be a king and a priest unto God," I said,
as I stood with mind attent, under a great fir-tree,
"it is this which gives honor unspeakable to the
sons of men, who will reach high rank, if not to-
day. To be forever with the Lord, to be in training for his service, this gives an unspeakable dignity to life."

And Helen, who stood by, listening to the songs

above, and who saw the pageantry of the moment, now said,—

"Did not our Lord bid the disciples rejoice, not so much in the subjection of spirits to their word, as to rejoice that their names were written in heaven?"

"Above all the glitter of earthly crowns, and the noise and tumult of the people," I said, "you see the world's true rulers, the heavenly kings,— with crowns unstained by blood and the tears of the innocent, and whose right to reign no revolution and no strong tyranny can disturb. And they will turn and overturn till he whose right it is shall come to reign over the nations as over the saints in the earth."

Then I went with my daughter along the mountain-side, crossing a deep ravine, to a point a little further to the west; and here, upon a plateau, or bench of the next mountain in the range, we found the morning fire of a great company of celestial soldiery,—and we saw their evolution in airy flight, as the sun was peering over the mountains on the east. These are they who sometimes engage in human battles. Their leader came forth, as fair as the morning,—he who had slain the hosts of the Assyrian king. And we heard their morning song: "The chariots of God are myriads of angels."

Now turning to the mountain-side southward,

far up the heights, yet still among the fir-trees,
we found the camp of those who are the ministers
of the Divine Vengeance. Here we saw those who
destroyed Sodom, and those who removed from
life the first-born of Egypt, those who smote by
pestilence in Jerusalem, and who slew Herod since
he gave not to God the glory.

Then passing swiftly across the area below, we
reached the mountain-sides upon the east, among
the dark firs; and under a frowning precipice
not yet illuminated by the sunbeams, we saw the
glowing fire of the Angels of the Judgment,—
who are, day by day, the instruments of God in
the closing scenes of every peopled sphere. And
we heard their solemn morning hymn, preceding their swift flight to realms afar, where they
were to do quickly the deeds of God, in closing
up the accounts of some distant globe :—

> This day, the Son of Man, on high, shall send
> His angels forth; they haste to gather out
> His kindom, all in guilt that do offend,
> And them that love and do iniquity.
> The Son of Man in brightest glory comes,—
> The Father's glory; and his angels reap
> The golden harvest ripe,—the end has come.
> The angel trumpet clang awakes the dead;
> The trumpet's joyful sound, from out four winds,
> Will gather all who seek atoning love.
> The Son of Man enrobed shall sit, and judge,—
> All nations calling to his righteous seat.

Discerning angels forth shall come ; the just
From unjust, severing right and left, from God :
And angel hands award the rightful doom
Pronounced by him, upon his throne of love.

CHAPTER FIFTH

I

THEN, as if we had the wings of the morning, we passed in swiftest flight afar, from out the amphitheatre, to the camp of the Angels of the Home. It was just below the great waterfalls of the river of Peace, where the broad stream drops from the horseshoe mountain plateau to the plains below. Here, amid the palms, we found their encampment, extending far upon each side of the stream east and west under the great northern wall of rock, and far down the shining river upon either bank.

The angel who led Eliezer to Mesopotamia, unto the city of Nahor, was he whom we saw in charge of the entire encampment of the Home Circle.

We first visited the right bank of the river, at some distance from the mist and the thunder of the waterfall, and here we found that Division that cares for the children in the Land of Shadows. Dr. Martin Luther was the leader of these guardian angels to-day. And we heard him say to a little company :—

"From early childhood, I would accustom a child, and say to it : 'Dear child, thou hast an angel of thine own. When thou prayest, morning and evening, the same angel will be with thee, and sit beside thy little bed, clothed in a white robe; will take care of thee, lull thee to sleep, and guard over thee that the evil one may not come near thee. So also when thou sayest the blessing and the thank-offering at thy meals, thine angel will be with thee at table, will serve thee, and guard thee.' If we pictured this to children from their earliest years, that angels are with them, this would not only make the dear children trust to the guardianship of the dear angels, but it would make them gentle and good, for they would think, 'If our parents are not here, the angels are here, and the evil one must not tempt us to do wrong.'"

Then we wandered here and there among the date-palms, conversing with those who thread so oft the avenue of great cities, mingling with the multitudes, and visiting lone homes,—always mindful of those children who shall be heirs of salvation.

The appearance of these beings was such that Helen could never weary of watching their busy goings to and fro, or their gathering in little groups to converse together.   The glory of their faces, and their gorgeous apparel, indicated that when they were not traversing the sin-stained earth, they were always beholding the face of our Father, as angels whose privilege it is to stand in the immediate presence of the Infinite Majesty.

II

Crossing over to the east bank we found, not far from the cliffs, amid the cocoanut-palms, the camp of the Bread Givers; in charge to-day of the archangel who ministered to Christ in the wilderness.

And here, too, was Elijah,—the peerless on earth, of rank in heaven,—coming hither to ask for those in sore distress for the necessities of life, the oil and the meal; and mindful of that angelic service, by which he was strengthened in desert wanderings.

A revered apostle, too, who had heard the Macedonian cry on earth, was here to-day,—ready to give, as once to receive, angelic suggestion.

"Give us this day our daily bread," we could see flying from the flag-staff, at headquarters. And we listened to earnest consultations concerning the underlying conditions of drought, or flood, of famine, or plenty, in the Land of Shadows.

III

Next passing down the left bank of the river at some remove, we found the encampment of the Sons of Consolation.

The camp-fire at headquarters was near a wide-spreading banyan-tree, that served as a hall of assembly for the vast company that extended widely west, rising over the second bank of the Peace, and whose tents were also seen afar over the green meadows down the river.

The angel who met Hagar in the wilderness was the leader of the Comforters. And "Thou God seest me," was upon their banner.

The most part of this company were those temporarily attached to the corps, for the purpose of standing close beside their earthly dear ones in their hours of personal bereavement.

Helen searched the records, and found my name there,—since I had been for some time in this service, and often absent from the heavens that I might stand by her who walks alone in a sun-lighted nook of the Land of Shadows. How often I have been there, she knows not; yet her prayers of faith and hope and love are heard by our Father, who answers them through one whom he sendeth.

Yet, when my daughter found the record, and

read the transcript of service, the tears welled
to her eyes, in thinking of her mother.   And
then she sang, in a minor key,—

> Cease thy mourning, child of sorrow,
>   All thy tears are wiped away:
> Not to-day, but on the morrow,
>   Light shall break in perfect day.
> List above,—the heavens rejoice ;
>   List ye to the angel's voice,—
>   "He comforts thee."

> Sing, exult, O child of sorrow,
>   See thine angel yet alive :
> Life the face of death did borrow,
>   Life thy home did so deprive.
> Rise from weeping, join the songs,—
>   "Glory to our God belongs:
>   He comforts thee."

IV

Now crossing over to the western river bank,
far below the camp of the Guardians of the Children, we saw amid a noble grove of fan-palms,
the camp-fire of those who go oft to the Land of
Shadows to visit the beds of the dying, to bring
them safely to these realms of light.   They
watch by sick-beds, in tender ministration ; and
they know the moment of release, when the

physical changes that accompany death enable the patient to perceive the spiritual presence of those who approach them in supernal light.

"The guides on the Alps," said Helen, "have been often over every step of the way, and can safely guide. So the angels often passing between the low earth and the high heavens can show us just how to plant our feet at every step, so as to reach our home at last."

He is master, to-day, in this department of service, who bore to the bosom of Abraham the beggar Lazarus, so rich in faith.

And over the silken folds of the official tent of Tyrian purple, we saw in letters of gold :—

"Bright angels are from glory come,
   They're round his bed, they're in his room;
   They wait to waft his spirit home:
                     All is well, all is well."

13

Book VI

THE MESSAGE OF THE ANGEL

•

CHAPTER FIRST

I

RETURNING now to the camp of the Angel of
the New Birth, we saw one, of my daughter's
age, speeding to meet her own Guardian Spirit,
just now returned from the old home on earth.
We heard their interchange of words, which
strangely touched the heart of Helen, who had
been here so little time :—

> " What news from home ?
> Where'er I roam,
> I think of earth—
> My place of birth."

> " Good news," the angel said, swift flying—
> A moment's flight from life with the dying.

> " I cannot quite forget my childhood lessons old,
> In studies new ; or homely house, in house of gold.
> O tell me, do they spend their days in sighing ?"

> " No, God has quenched their tears, and stilled their
>   crying ;
> No discord mars their earthly psalm :
> Your home is filled with holy calm."

"O do they keep their hearth-fire glowing ?
 Is life with even current flowing ?"

"Their grief is strangely past my sounding,
 The oil of joy is in their wounding ;
 How deep their woe
 I cannot know.
The fires are bright,—the hearth-stone never yet was
 cold ;
And life moves on, as if you ne'er had left their fold."

"O angel swift, there is, I know, a vacant place ;
 You say that, day by day, 'tis filled by heavenly grace:
 Their empty hearts would strongly cry,
 Unless to rescue them you fly.
 With eager heart I seek to know
 How I may help their life below ;
 I long to learn the heavenly lore
 By which to bind the hearts now sore ;
 To fit myself to fill your place,
 To wipe all tears from sorrow's face."

Then Helen said,—" I can hardly restrain my tears, when I think of home. Our God is a Comforter; yet mother and sister are human. If I can but go and sit beside them, and silently sympathize with them, it will do me good; and sometime perhaps I can learn how to help them in some better way. Let me, therefore, at once hasten back to my place in the Training School; for I am but a novice in any art of heavenly ministration."

In turning, Helen met her Guardian Angel, whom she had never seen before; yet one who had never ceased to watch her earthly years. And after some moments, in exchange of greetings, my daughter said :—

"I am eager, O Angel love, to tell my kin in the Land of Shadow, how bright is the Light of our Father's House; and speak to some I know, of the power of an endless life, that they may set their affections on things above. But I cannot make my message known. Not yet have I waxed strong in spirit, to venture flight so far; nor have I learned the psychic laws by which I may approach the friends I love and all who are of willing heart, to tell my tale of light and life supernal."

"Give me thy message, child."

And in a moment more, with first a parting word to me, they went away together to the school for teaching those who desire to minister in the Land of Shadows.

CHAPTER SECOND

ERE long the twilight fires were kindled; and little knots soon gathered here and there throughout the entire encampment, and some who'd had a long experience in service began to tell their tales of earth and heaven. As I was moving past the tent of him who led these hosts, I noted that here too some were rehearsing the stories of distant worlds, or far-off ages. As I paused to listen, I heard one say :—

"Since Jesus was born as a little babe in Bethlehem, I have never ceased to visit the earth, to help mothers care for their babes. And oft I change my work by God's appointment, and watch the tender years of youth. Of late, for a score of years, I've had one charge, now finished, —of which I will briefly tell the story.

I

"All my pride of ancient years in heaven, my rank and honors won before the earth was formed or stars created, I have placed at the service of a little child; sometimes a poor man's child, and often a child diseased or deformed, that he might become rich towards God, and the heir of salvation. Who am I that I should do less,—since I serve those for whom Christ died. A few thousand years out of an endless life, is time well spent, if I may bring many sons unto glory.

"O myriad hosts of God, ye who, in numbers without number, never sinned, not from the heavenly standpoint can ye know the beauty of a child divine in realms of evil. As one who has, for ages, sought to solve the mysteries of mind, to understand its beginnings and unfoldings, and its relation to the Infinite, I have for nineteen centuries watched the babes and youth of the Land of Shadows. Virtues here so common that we never notice them, are there so rare that all men notice them.

"So when my task of love was finished, it was said, concerning her whom I served, that she was unselfish, that there never was a time when she was not first of all thoughtful of others. It was as if she had been born in heaven. And from the beginning, through all her years, the angels, who walked that way, said,—'She is one of us.' And early they claimed their own.

"'Tis trifling to tell the tale, yet it is to us unique. I saw my blessed child, in the bloom of early womanhood, walk far over roads that needed to be paved with gold to be fairly passable, to visit maidens of threescore years and ten, poor, and infirm in body and broken in mind, that she might cheer their hearts and their lips by love, where love was needed to gladden their lives.

"It is trifling to tell the tale, but she yielded precious hours, in her bright and cheery youth, for hearing woe-begone stories of aged distress, when no one else would hear them. If there was no one else to bear to a darkened house the light, she carried it like a ministering angel, casting sunshine wherever she went.

"Peculiar and alone, disappointed and poor, vicious and blameworthy, was the old man, living far from her home, to whom she made errands of mercy,—since there was no one to love him.

"And when a sweet-voiced mother sang her songs with a far-away look, as if her angel child were listening; and when to her the birds of June seemed to sing in a sad and lonely strain, as if they too had a great sorrow,—as if all nature were grieving when her musical child took his flight into realms ethereal and unknown,—it was then that I saw my charge, in the dawn and hope and upspringing life of youth, take up the burden of woe and make it her own, seeking to make bearable that which she could not understand, seeking to express in childlike words the great love of the Infinite Father, and the sympathy of the Man of Sorrows.

"In domestic poverty, with its endless chagrins, she maintained her sweetness of spirit. Willing in humble duties, and restless under toils imposed when worse than useless; swift of thought, and patient to plod where need required; with broken and pinched-up years of schooling, she shaped her work to toil, to earn, to serve the Master's will, with a physical organization no match for the needs of the hour.

"Yet, to her the earth was little else than heaven. The sea, the sea, she loved the sea. Wild forest paths, the green-armed pines, the drooping firs, the sturdy oaks, the weeping elms, —she took them to her heart. She loved to be alone in solitudes unsafe upon the sinful earth, and I am glad to have her here in these fair wildernesses of God.

"The hoar antiquity of man's thought on God, his worship on a thousand hills of earth, old forms of prayer, the sacred words of saints in bygone ages,—these types of moral life gave strength for her daily battle.

II

" 'It is a strange story to us who have had so many years in heaven, yet I saw my precious child, when she walked for miles beside the sea, bearing her Sunday shoes in her hand till near the church,—yet her soul in perfect tune with the sweet bells and hymns of praise, and all singing angels of earth or heaven ; and then I saw her after the service seated by a gray-and-green wall, with moss and vines, and the breath of the sea,—and there she wrote :—

" ' Be it remembered that, here and now, I seek the grace and aid of the most merciful God and Father :

" ' To the end that I may be conformed to the perfect pattern in absolute goodness, in absolute sincerity and regard for the truth and honor, thinking no evil, having an appreciation of all values, being absolutely loyal to God, home, friends, duty, and the best interests ;

" ' To the end that I may forget self, and be made perfect in love ; that I may be lifted out of all smallness and meanness of mind and soul, and enlarged to such proportions as the Divine Architect would fain see ; that I may be free from any jealousy, envy, and malice, and un-charitableness, and petty conceits ;

"'That I may never fear the truth, or be prejudiced, or restricted in my view of any thing or person by personal spite or one-sidedness, but that I may be able to look at things on all sides without fear, and with impartiality, justice, and charity:

"'And deliver me, O Lord, above all things, from my own self-conceit and self-love;

"'Help me to bear with the smallness and infirmity and jealousy and narrow-mindedness of others, and all their petty faults,—and help me not to judge others, that Thou in Thy mercy mayest spare me; grant that I may not despise any of Thy creatures;

"'Help me in seeking to arouse the divine spark — that which is godlike in people; that Thou wouldst teach me, that I may help those poor half-alive people to truly live; that with Thine aid I may bear a little—at least a little— light to those who sit in darkness, and in the shadow of death; that I may help them to preserve the life energy; that Thou wouldst so fill me with the rapture of life in Thy glorious world that others may see Thee and the beauty of life and nature;

"'That I may never be bound by the sordid things of earth, or become slothful, and bound by fleshly lusts, but that with Thine aid I may

with grace and humility glorify the common
life, and make life beautiful;

"'That I may be kept from wounding any,
and from sin by carelessness of speech:

"'O Father, I am so very weak and despicable,
I can hope to accomplish nothing unless I am
very close to Thee: O Lord, do Thou remember
me; O Lamb of God, that takest away the sins
of the world, have mercy on me. Amen.'

III

"She was an eager child, with heart of fire,—
consuming all things that would offend the highest honor; and impatient of all within herself
that needed mending; a modest, shrinking
child, well balanced, yet deeply bemoaning all
the imperfections incident to her immaturity, in
plan and achievement. Yet her life matured in
the ripening of moral character.

"And now it was, that our Father directed
her removal,—since her physical organization
and temperament were ill-fitted for length of
earthly days, unless by bodily distress and woe.
Life's chief aim, for her, was better to be served
here, than there.

"I told her our Father's voice and call: and
at first she said,—'There are so many suffering

and poor in the world, I wanted to help them ;'
then next she said,—'Our Father knows the best.'

"And as she sought to live, so she sought to
die, with angelic sweetness of daily disposition ;
having such sense of the proprieties of a life related to immortal destiny, that it seemed to her
ill befitting the dignity of her spiritual nature to
complain of her lot, or to manifest the slightest
sense of inconvenience amid the untold chagrins
of failing physical powers.

"And one bright June day she said, 'I have
felt, to-day, that the next journey I make I will
go to the heavenly country.'

"And the next day, she said, 'I trust in
Christ alone, whose blood avails for me.' And
then she passed through the gates of the morning, and reached the endless day.

"I have told this tale, my lord, and my comrades who seek the world's redemption, to illustrate my clear and unmistakable testimony, that
oft the light of God illumines the Land of Shadows ; and there are multitudes of youth, in every
generation, whose great characteristic it is, that
they are pure in heart, and that they will see
God.   This elevates the moral tone of the whole
world out of which they hasten.   'Their spirits
go, as sinks the sun to rest, noiselessly, peace-
fully, but leaving a sky brilliant with the hues
of faith and hope.'

"To be of the smallest service to these heirs of salvation, carries with it its own reward,—an unspeakable reward in all the future ages of those who are so redeemed from out the Land of Shadow, and who are brought safely home to the Light of our Father's House.

"Yet, my lord, this precious child and charge, over whom I have watched for a score of years, has never seen my face, until to-day. And, for her sake, and for my sake, and for the glory of our common Lord and Master, I ask you another sitting, at the next twilight camp-fire.

"O ye, who seek the sculptor's art, or skill in depicting life by brush and form and color—there is no work more worthy the ambition of angels than this : to go far hence to the shadow of lands that know not God—there to find the plastic mind of some little child, there to shape and mould the spirit, till it is fitted to beautify the earth and to gladden the realms of bliss."

CHAPTER THIRD

WHEN fell the evening hour, when flashed the heavenly rings of light that belt celestial spheres, when glowed the lights of planets near, when fell the light of many moons—when twilight reigned in heaven where there is no night—then the camp-fire burned; and the Angel swift, who loud proclaims the Gospel in trumpet tones o'er earth, now gathered messengers to hear the Guardian's tale.

"A faithful witness I have found. Not yet, my lord, and comrades all, is the messenger prepared to go, not being yet of skill to gain an earthly hearing. Yet to me my charge has spoken,—'Will not some of you who know, my message tell, O tell the earthly people. It is burning in my heart to say: write, O write, my angel love.'

"And, my lord, I sought some other service, yet the Master bade me do this. My sainted child has brought from earth intense insistence; urging so, that I cannot shake it off. And since our Master wills it, I will give you the message.

14

"'I should like to put an idea into their heads to do it,' my charge has spoken. 'I should think that men would be glad to do, to give, to make the earth like heaven. And I wish that I could put an idea into their heads to do it.

"'I would say to all who dwell in the Land of Shadows, that, if you could know how bright is the Light of our Father's House, you would attempt to make the beloved earth like heaven— you would live like the angels of God.

"'Our Lord has said that Moses and the prophets are enough, without raising witness from the dead. If it be little you can know, then know well that little.

"'What I would have, O earthly Church beloved, thou bride of the Heavenly Bridegroom, is this : that you have the same faith in what Moses and the prophets and our Lord and his apostles have said about heaven and the stirring life of angel hosts, that you have in other things revealed in the Word of God. There are two hundred and fifty texts in the Bible upon this point, that set forth the mind of the Spirit ; and the Holy One intended to teach that which relates to the highest spiritual good of the people of God. The Church needs to give greater prominence, and to hold in firmer and more vivid and more rational belief, that which relates to our Home in glory.

"'Has not the historic manifestation of Jesus Christ been the one great boon of earth? His unique relation to mankind ought, then, to give our Lord a hearing in his testimony about heaven and the angels. There is no need of other witness:—"I am from above;" "In my Father's house;" "I go to prepare a place." The words of Jesus are solid, to build upon. There is no need to go through life, or to stand by graves, saying, —"If."

"'The power of the world to come, ought to be felt as a popular power in the Church of God. Materialists and agnostics have no right to make Christianity cautious of giving prominence to the solid reality of the heavenly state,—so far as the Bible text has revealed it. "While we attempt," said Dr. Chalmers, "not to be wise above that which is written, we should attempt, and that most studiously, to be wise up to that which is written." And Archbishop Whately has said, that because little is revealed in regard to the heavenly state, the Church of God should endeavor so to dwell on the points that are revealed, as to make the most of what little knowledge we do have.

"'What the Church has, is knowledge, positive and clear; and not ignorance, and not doubt. It

is a wholesome influence to make the vision of
heaven more vivid.   Men live on a low plane ;
too low, for those whose children are to-day in
heaven.

"'The power of the world to come needs to be
felt in every household and counting-room, in
every shop and field.   The world stands in need
to-day of a revival, all-sweeping, of a practical
belief in immortality.   Men ought to-day, to live
like the angels of God ; and to be actuated by
heavenly motives, in every hour of their lives.

"'The time is certainly coming in which people will know that 'To him that knoweth to do
good, and doeth it not, to him it is sin.'   The
great evil is slothfulness.   People have aspiration for a higher life, then forget it.   They attend church, their souls are stirred by a mo-
mentary impulse ; then they eat the Sunday din-
ner, and lapse into their former state.   The
trouble is, they do not see ; if they could see,
they would act.

II

"'Your guardian angels, O men of earth, are
calling in sweet tones, like bells from out the
eternal world.   Can you, to-day, look your Guardian Angel in the face without a blush ?   May
not the accents of angelic language be heard

upon the earth? Your mother, sister, wife, child, may be speaking to you at this moment.

"'It is not going to be the same with you, whatever you do, or fail to do. Near Monadnock mountain, was born one of the most influential men in the modern Church. His mate, of equal intellectual powers, wasted his life till he was seventy years old. It can never be the same with those two men, to all eternity.

"'O ye men who are clear of vision, know ye that the heavenly state is no vague and uncertain condition that will not bear to be inquired into. It is as solid as the sun, the planets, the varied spheres of God. Force is never lost, it is transferred in change, it is transformed, it is indestructible. If materialists bid men believe that nature is abiding, why not by parity of reasoning believe that the thinking part of nature is undying?

"'Life originates somehow in connection with cosmic ether, or it is vitally connected with it; and it continues to exist in higher forms, after the body has fallen to pieces. So that, in dying, as we call it, the ridding ourselves of the body, the undying force the soul merely passes beyond the visual horizon. It sails, as one has said, off soundings. Your life is like an ocean current, cutting its way straight onward, through the world of waters. Your present career will be continued in the eternal world. Moral character abides. In essential character, Gabriel is not different from an earthly child of God.

"'We know that upon the earth we inherit a certain disposition from our ancestors, that it is impossible for us to shake off. So in the life unending, we inherit something of the character we ourselves had upon the earth; and thus our early life is perpetuated in the unseen. The spiritual body of the unseen world is intensely individualized, the outgrowth of the personal character gained on earth; as a man's body is the outgrowth of the physical and moral character of his ancestors. These points are well made, by thoughtful men; and they are reasonable.

III

"'The ordinary life, therefore, of all men ought to be surcharged with the august thought of personal immortality. The perspective of life is altered, when viewed from the standpoint of the unseen world. The aspect of human society is widened and changed by opening up the outlying heavenly horizon; so that men may discern things in their true proportion by the light cast upon them from out the eternal world.

"'In view of his own timeless relations to the world unseen, every man ought to walk like a sovereign from some superior realm. He ought to be above doing that which is unworthy. The radiant hope of immortality should light up all dark corners in the Land of Shadows. Men ought to become accustomed to the thought of a superior life, and to be actuated by motives drawn from it; as they are accustomed to deal with unseen continents on earth. Friendships and business pursuits should be measured by their relation to the future of the soul. Noble lives are controlled, shaped, guided, from out the unseen. And this must be so, since only a few moments of time remain, and then eternal ages come on apace, and on they roll forever.

IV

"'Every street in the city of gold, says my old teacher, begins on earth. Do not live, merely wishing—only to die despairing. Do not seek merely to paint yourselves into glory, as that emperor did, who had his portrait painted as he would appear in heaven.

"'God has hung out many lights to guide you into the everlasting rest. Heed the lights.

"'The heavens sing a song of joy when a man is born again, and becomes God's child. And he is watched over by angelic ministry, which guides him home at last.

V

" ' Dwelling in the presence of a lofty life, with heaven bending over you, open your hearts, O mournful tribes of men, to the light of a better world. In ceaseless storms of grief, run to God with all your sorrows. The only abiding relief in wretchedness is the presence of the Divine Comforter.

" ' I needed to have my own life plan shocked by the Death Angel : God had his plan in my outgoing. A foot-breadth, tangible, of heavenly soil, is worth more than immeasurable leagues of earth.

" ' O mourning one, dream no more of buds removed, or broken columns, for life is not marred by death. Death is for perfect blooming, or better building. It is completion, it is triumph. There is no blight, or imperfection, or prematurity of removal, in passing on from life to life.

" ' If the Lord opens these heavenly gates, and calls, who would not gladly go; dropping instantly all favorite pursuits, all earthly hopes and aspirations, and unfinished plans, and, bidding godspeed for a day to earthly companions, seek henceforth the heavenly? Welcome, heaven.

" ' Here, in heaven, we congratulate each other

when we hear that our friends are about to die. Be glad, O child of earth, if you have mortal tokens that presage immortality.

VI

"'Mystery after mystery is swift unfolding. Now, O men of earth, ye know how the eye of God penetrates the walls of every house, that no height nor depth can hide from him, and how, too, your Guardian Angel reads your thought. Lift your eyes a little higher, and know that heaven unseen is the true coronation of life.

"'Yet the heavenly crown is not of gold, it is a crown of character—a character whole, holy. Heaven is first of all a character, then a place.

"'O ye, who are conscious of imperfect lives, of lives lacking in perfect love to God and man, know ye that the sons and daughters of the Almighty need to form the mind anew,—to put on the purpose and habit, or clothing, of love; and need to confide in the mercy of him who casts over the penitent his righteous robe. So we wash our robes and make them clean, and we sing a new song :—

"'Blessed be the God and Father of our Lord Jesus Christ, who hath blessed us with every spiritual blessing:

" ' And this is his commandment, that we should believe in the name of his son Jesus Christ :

" ' In whom we have redemption through his blood, the forgiveness of our trespasses :

" ' Wherefore also he is able to save to the uttermost them that draw near unto God through him." '

VII

Now when the Guardian Angel had told this message, and asked who would bear it to the Land of Shadow, many were they who answered, —" Here am I, send me."

CHAPTER FOURTH

WHEN next I saw my daughter, she said,—
"Now, I have my own room in our Father's house."

And when next I saw her, she said,—"Mother has come, and sister has come; and now we shall all be together again."

THE END